GW00992055

DRAMA COLLECTION
WITHAM LIBRARY
18 NEWLAND STREET
WITHAM, ESSEX CM8 2AQ

L HQ/DRA

01. 05.

27. 07. 93

13. 02. 95

11 DEC 1997

This book is to be returned on or before the date above.
It may be borrowed for a further period if not in demand.

HW52088

LIBRARIES

FEMALE TRANSPORT

by

STEVE GOOCH

SAMUEL FRENCH, INC.
45 WEST 25TH STREET   NEW YORK 10010
7623 SUNSET BOULEVARD HOLLYWOOD 90046
LONDON   TORONTO

Copyright © 1974 by Steve Gooch

ALL RIGHTS RESERVED

*CAUTION: Professionals and amateurs are hereby warned that FEMALE
TRANSPORT is subject to a royalty. It is fully protected under the copyright laws
of the United States of America, the British Commonwealth, including Canada, and
all other countries of the Copyright Union. All rights, including professional,
amateur, motion pictures, recitation, lecturing, public reading, radio broadcasting,
television, and the rights of translation into foreign languages are strictly reserved.
In its present form the play is dedicated to the reading public only.*

*The amateur live stage performance rights to FEMALE TRANSPORT are
controlled exclusively by Samuel French, Inc., and royalty arrangements and
licenses must be secured well in advance of presentation. PLEASE NOTE that
amateur royalty fees are set upon application in accordance with your producing
circumstances. When applying for a royalty quotation and license please give us the
number of performances intended, dates of production, your seating capacity and
admission fee. Royalties are payable one week before the opening performance of
the play to Samuel French, Inc., at 45 W. 25th Street, New York, NY 10010; or at
7623 Sunset Blvd., Hollywood, CA 90046, or to Samuel French (Canada), Ltd., 80
Richmond Street East, Toronto, Ontario, Canada M5C 1P1.*

*Royalty of the required amount must be paid whether the play is presented
for charity or gain and whether or not admission is charged.*

Stock royalty quoted on application to Samuel French, Inc.

*For all other rights than those stipulated above, apply to Margaret Ramsay
Ltd., 14a Goodwin's Court, St. Martins Lane, London WC2N 4LL, England.*

*Particular emphasis is laid on the question of amateur or professional
readings, permission and terms for which must be secured in writing from Samuel
French, Inc.*

*Copying from this book in whole or in part is strictly forbidden by law, and
the right of performance is not transferable.*

*Whenever the play is produced the following notice must appear on all
programs, printing and advertising for the play: "Produced by special arrangement
with Samuel French, Inc."*

*Due authorship credit must be given on all programs, printing and
advertising for the play.*

ISBN 0 573 69185 1   Printed in U.S.A.

ESSEX COUNTY LIBRARY

HW52088

No one shall commit or authorize any act or omission by which the copyright of, or the right to copyright, this play may be impaired.

No one shall make any changes in this play for the purpose of production.

Publication of this play does not imply availability for performance. Both amateurs and professionals considering a production are *strongly* advised in their own interests to apply to Samuel French, Inc., for written permission before starting rehearsals, advertising, or booking a theatre.

No part of this book may be reproduced, stored in a retrieval system, or transmitted in any form, by any means, now known or yet to be invented, including mechanical, electronic, photocopying, recording, videotaping, or otherwise, without the prior written permission of the publisher.

IMPORTANT BILLING AND CREDIT REQUIREMENTS

All producers of FEMALE TRANSPORT *must* give credit to the Author of the Play in all programs distributed in connection with performances of the Play and in all instances in which the title of the Play appears for purposes of advertising, publicizing or otherwise exploiting the Play and/or a production. The name of the Author *must* also appear on a separate line, on which no other name appears, immediately following the title, and *must* appear in size of type not less than fifty percent the size of the title type.

FEMALE TRANSPORT was given its premiere at the Half Moon Theatre, London, on 15 November 1973. Directed by Ron Daniels, designed by Andy Montag, it had the following cast:

WINNIE............................... Ann Holloway
MADGE .... Yvonne Gilan
NANCE............................... Kate Crutchley
PITTY............................... Anthea Meadows
SARAH...................................June Page
CHARLOTTE......................Aviva Goldkorn
TOMMY .... Billy Colvill
SARGE................................. Charles Cork
CAPTAIN ....Michael Irving
SURGEON..............................Alan David

AUTHOR'S NOTE

Female Transport was given its first performance at the Half Moon Theatre, a 100-seater community theatre in Alie Street, London E1. The Half Moon isn't a rich theatre and, because of its size and shape, it has its own "scruffy" intimate atmosphere. It is also a totally flexible auditorium, so the play was performed as near in-the-round as was possible, with the audience on three long sides. The "above-deck" scenes were played literally above the audience on a platform ten feet over their heads. Although it should be possible to produce the play anywhere this kind of environmental staging in the kind of auditorium and atmosphere described above is particularly well-suited to the play.

Also, it is not a literary piece but primarily a verbal or oral one. It would be essential therefore for a production to attempt to capture the accent and syntax of a working-class dialect. For the same reason it is desirable for the performers to be more than just familiar with the same oral style. Apart from this, as is obvious from the text, the play should be particularly well-suited to companies well-versed in group theatre and the performance of new texts to community audiences.

Any book of Australian folk songs will give music suitable for the songs in this play.

A cell.
Two large beds, a stove, two buckets.

(WINNIE, NANCE, MADGE, PITTY, CHARLOTTE and
    SARAH come on, in chains. Outside the cell they sing
    "Botany Bay.")*

    GIRLS.
FAREWELL TO OLD ENGLAND FOR EVER
FAREWELL TO MY RUM CALLS AS WELL
FAREWELL TO THE WELL-KNOWN OLD BAILEY
WHERE I USED TO CUT SUCH A SWELL.

THERE'S THE CAPTAIN AS IS OUR COMMANDER
THERE'S THE SURGEON AND ALL THE SHIP'S
CREW
NOT THE FIRST BUT THE SECOND-CLASS
PASSENGERS
KNOWS WHAT WE POOR CONVICTS GO THROUGH

TAIN'T LEAVING OLD ENGLAND WE CARE ABOUT
TAIN'T COS WE MIS-SPELLS WHAT WE KNOWS
BUT BECAUSE ALL WE LIGHT-FINGERED GENTRY
HOPS AROUND WITH A LOG ON OUR TOES.

FOR FOURTEEN LONG YEARS I AM SENTENCED
FOR FOURTEEN LONG YEARS AND A DAY
FOR MEETING A BLOKE IN THE AREA

---

*See p. 95 for music.

7

AND SNEAKING HIS TICKER AWAY.

OH HAD I THE WINGS OF A TURTLE-DOVE
I'D SOAR ON MY PINIONS SO HIGH
SLAP BANG TO THE ARMS OF MY POLLY LOVE
AND IN HER SWEET PRESENCE I'D DIE.

(*SARGE and TOMMY come on. They let the girls into
the cell. Each of them has a small bag of personal
belongings.*)

WINNIE. Spacious, en it.
SARGE. No talkin'!
NANCE. Better'n Newgate, darlin'.
SARGE. You 'eard me!
NANCE. Sod off.

(*SARGE pins NANCE to the wall with a baton against her
throat. NANCE kicks. SARGE dodges. CHARLOTTE
starts a chant. The other girls join in.*)

CHARLOTTE. Oi! Oi! Oi! Oi! Oi!

(*Etcetera, until SARGE, releasing NANCE, says:*)

SARGE. ALL RIGHT!

(*The girls fall silent. NANCE holds her throat.*)

SARGE. I ain' avin' that.
CHARLOTTE. An' we ain' 'avin' that.
NANCE. (*Taking out a hairpin.*) Try that again, I'll
ram this up yer cock.
SARGE. I'll 'ave that. (*He holds out his hand.*)
NANCE. Get stuffed.

SARGE. I'll remember you two.
CHARLOTTE. You do that.
SARGE. You first.

(*He goes to chain NANCE up. She doesn't cooperate.*)

SARGE. It's got a be done.
CHARLOTTE. Go on, girl.

(*NANCE acquiesces. SARGE chains her up. TOMMY chains up WINNIE.*)

WINNIE. All mod cons, I see.
CHARLOTTE. Least they don't pin yer legs t'gether.
WINNIE. They did my brother. Shufflin' Wonder they called 'im.
SARAH. Your brother was Jesus fuckin' Christ.
WINNIE. One a the first out, my brother.
CHARLOTTE. Jus' means 'e got caught sooner.

(*SARGE and TOMMY move on to MADGE and SARAH.*)

WINNIE. Knight a the road 'e was. Worked the 'ighways. Kep' the 'ole fam'ly, good as. We all looked up to 'im. Never went without when 'e was 'ome. A real gent. Taught me shopliftin'. Took me down the market one Saturday, made me put this big skirt on. I was only six. People kep' lookin' at me. 'Ah, en she sweet,' they said. I'ad enough fresh fruit up me knickers t'feed the family a fortnight.
SARAH. You an' your fam'ly.
WINNIE. Jus' cos you never 'ad one.

(*SARGE and TOMMY move on to PITTY and CHARLOTTE.*)

PITTY. Please, I don' wan' a go.
SARGE. No good tellin' me, darlin'.
SARAH. 'Oo is she?
PITTY. I'm ill.
CHARLOTTE. Yer always get one.
SARAH. Whass the matter with 'er?
WINNIE. God knows.
PITTY. I'll die on the journey!
NANCE. You won't be the only one, darlin'.
PITTY. It's a mistake.
CHARLOTTE. We all say that, sweet'eart.
SARAH. Be a right drag with 'er.
CHARLOTTE. Can't we get rid of 'er?
MADGE. 'Old your noise!
PITTY. I told 'em I weren't well.
MADGE. I'll see yer're all right, love. (*She puts her hand on PITTY's shoulder.*)
WINNIE. Watch 'er!

(*PITTY whimpers and buries her head in MADGE's lap.*)

SARAH. Too late.
CHARLOTTE. Fast mover, en't yer.
MADGE. Mind yer own.
SARGE. Anythin' else yer need, ask the lad. Tommy's 'is name.
SARAH. Nice.
WINNIE. You've embarrassed 'im.

(*SARGE and TOMMY go. Pause.*)

WINNIE. Stuffy, en it.

NANCE. Wait till we been at sea a few weeks. More'n a 'undred of us in this tub. Place'll stink like a fuckin' bull-market.

CHARLOTTE. Cow-market.

MADGE. And you.

NANCE. (*Pause.*) Cou'nt believe it on the coach from the 'Ulks. Fresh air so pure I cou'nt smell it. Cou'nt appreciate it.

WINNIE. (*Long pause.*) Quiet, en it.

SARAH. Gives yer the creeps.

SARAH. (*Pause.*) 'Ow long's it take?

WINNIE. Six months.

SARAH. Christ.

WINNIE. 'Undred an' fifty-one days the fastest so far.

CHARLOTTE. Walkin' lexicon, this one.

WINNIE. I made a study when me brother got sent.

MADGE. They keep these on yer all the time? (*The chains.*)

WINNIE. Depends if yer're good.

SARAH. I'm good.

CHARLOTTE. Fer a night.

SARAH. Thass more'n some.

NANCE. They're goin' a wan' proof a goodness.

WINNIE. 'S why women's ships take longest. Time all the guards get up all the prisoners.

SARAH. They do that?

WINNIE. Can't see 'em no tryin'.

CHARLOTTE. (*Pause.*) We get let out at all?

WINNIE. Reg'lar exercise. It's stip'lated.

NANCE. 'Ow often?

WINNIE. Twice a day's been known.

NANCE. Better'n on land.

WINNIE. This is tougher though.

MADGE. Anyone get seasick?

(No one knows.)

MADGE. Find out soon enough.

CHARLOTTE. Don't wan' 'Eart's Delight pukin' in yer lap, do yer.

MADGE. Why don't you stop pretendin' an' shove your evil tongue up your pretty girl friend's 'ole.

(Dead silence. CHARLOTTE gets up and goes as far as her chains will allow. She can't reach MADGE, who evades her.)

CHARLOTTE. I'll 'ave your eyes out.

MADGE. *(Ironic, clawing like a cat.)* Rrrr!

NANCE. 'Ow is she?

(MADE shrugs. Pause.)

WINNIE. Whass that thing yer get when the water's bad?

NANCE. Typhus.

WINNIE. Yer get that sometimes. Dysentery. Small-pox. Run through the 'ole ship.

SARAH. Cheerful, en't she.

WINNIE. It's better now they got medicals.

SARAH. I ain' 'ad no medical.

MADGE. None of us did.

NANCE. We better 'ad then, 'adn't we.

CHARLOTTE. Goin' a twist their arm, are yer?

Scene 2

The CAPTAIN, at the table, talks to the SURGEON.

CAPTAIN. Will you come or not?

SURGEON. That depends what you pay.

CAPTAIN. Fifty for the journey. Ten every month over six we're at sea.

SURGEON. I'm afraid that won't do.

CAPTAIN. It does the Navy.

SURGEON. I'm no longer with the Navy. I resigned my commission after my last tour of duty.

CAPTAIN. Why d'you want to come then?

SURGEON. It's not a question of wanting. As a freelance without friends in the Admiralty or the Medical Association one has to shift for oneself. Admirals' sons don't do this kind of work.

CAPTAIN. Look, I've got a makeshift crew, a rabble of mercenaries for a guard, no surgeon, and two days before we sail.

SURGEON. I'm afraid that's your problem.

CAPTAIN. Why wouldn't the other bloke come?

SURGEON. He hasn't been paid for his last voyage. He's written to the Navy Board three times but there's been no answer. Once he's at sea he won't be able to collect for another year. If he dies at sea the Board saves a large debt. He's staying in England till they cough up.

CAPTAIN. Can't they force him?

SURGEON. They're not really interested. In peacetime the Navy has a surplus of surgeons. It's hard to find a use for them and their market value is low. So just as the Government is dumping its surplus criminality in New South Wales now America's no longer available, so the Navy's dumping its surplus medical expertise on the ships that take it there. The Transport Service has been getting us on the cheap.

CAPTAIN. I'm not supposed to sail without a surgeon.

SURGEON. No one'll cry if you don't.

CAPTAIN. I can't offer you any more. I'll be lucky if I cover my costs.

SURGEON. I don't believe that.

CAPTAIN. I've got to make on this trip myself, you know! They've also been getting me on the cheap. That's why they prefer old boats. Till there's a disaster or a scandal. What are you asking?

SURGEON. A hundred for the voyage. Twenty every month over six.

CAPTAIN. Not on.

SURGEON. I've drawn up a contract. (*He takes it out.*) Complete authority in all matters concerning prisoners' health and well being. Proper living quarters, sleeping, washing and cleaning facilities. Good clothing and ventilation. Full and healthy diet. No excessive punishment. Full medical supplies and equipment. Seniority over the Captain of the Guard.

CAPTAIN. Sergeant.

SURGEON. I'm sorry?

CAPTAIN. Sergeant of the Guard. We couldn't get an officer.

SURGEON. I'll change that. (*He writes.*)

CAPTAIN. I can't pay what you ask.

SURGEON. Women are harder work, you know.

CAPTAIN. I dare say. Will you look them over before you go?

SURGEON. How many are there?

CAPTAIN. A hundred and three.

SURGEON. My fee would be five pounds.

CAPTAIN. I'll show you where they live.

Scene 3

The cell.
WINNIE, MADGE, PITTY, CHARLOTTE NANCE and
SARAH.

SARAH. 'Ere, Charlotte, 'oo's she remind yer of?
CHARLOTTE. 'Oo?
SARAH. Wiltin' Petal there.
CHARLOTTE. No?
SARAH. Look then!
CHARLOTTE. I'm lookin.
SARAH. The nose.
CHARLOTTE. I can see the nose.
SARAH. Comes on, sticks out a mile.
CHARLOTTE. I can see that.
PITTY. Don't please.
NANCE. Ol' Pitty?
SARAH. She guessed it!
PITTY. Please.
WINNIE. I don't get it.
NANCE. She looks like Pitt.
WINNIE. 'Oo's 'e?
CHARLOTTE. Prime Minister.
NANCE. Not any more 'e ain't. It's the Duke a
Portland now.
WINNIE. Nah, thass the name a the men's ship. I seen
it tied up aside our'n.
CHARLOTTE. The ship, my darlin', is named after the
Prime Minister.
WINNIE. Oh.
SARAH. 'Ere, what 'appens if the blokes' ship ain't
big enough fer all of 'em?

CHARLOTTE. Fit a couple in 'ere. (*She pats the bed under her skirt.*)

SARAH. Where? Under there? (*She lifts CHARLOTTE's skirt.*) Less 'ave a look!

CHARLOTTE. Get off!

PITTY. YOU BITCHES! BITCHES!

CHARLOTTE. (*Pause.*) Now, now, Pitty.

MADGE. They called 'er that on the 'Ulks. Count of 'er nose. Said she was Pitt's bastard daughter, the cows. Never bothered with 'er real name.

PITTY. KATHLEEN.

MADGE. All right, Kathleen.

NANCE. (*Pause.*) I 'eard we was goin' direct.

SARAH. Whass that?

NANCE. Not stoppin' nowhere.

CHARLOTTE. Long way without a piss-call.

WINNIE. We'll get scurvy.

SARAH. Whass that?

WINNIE. Yer teeth drop out.

SARAH. Jus' like that?

WINNIE. No fresh veg if yer don't stop. They'll probably give us somethin'. Lemon tea with sugar.

SARAH. I don't take sugar.

NANCE. Yer will now.

CHARLOTTE. You tellin' 'er?

SARAH. Soun's nice though, lemon tea with sugar.

CHARLOTTE. Every day fer six months?

SARAH. Some things you got a accep'.

NANCE. Not in 'ere darlin'. Don' accep' nothin'.

CHARLOTTE. Like not seein' a man fer six months. Fer some of us thass an 'ardship.

MADGE. Whass that supposed t' mean?

CHARLOTTE. You're usin' that girl.

MADGE. (*To PITTY.*) Am I usin' you, darlin'?

(*PITTY, in MADGE's lap, sticks her thumb in her mouth.*)

MADGE. Anyone think yer'd never seen it before.

NANCE. Start acceptin' now, we'll be middle aged before we're thirty.

WINNIE. Go mad if yer fret all the time, Nance.

NANCE. Go sane more like. Thass what they're frightened of.

(*SARGE and SURGEON appear outside the cell.*)

SARGE. Medical examination!

CHARLOTTE. Knickers down, girls!

(*The men come into the cell.*)

SURGEON. That won't be necessary.

NANCE. Bloody well ought a be. 'Alf of 'em on this ship's riddled with clap. I ain' gettin' it without a reason.

SURGEON. One seldom does. (*To WINNIE.*) Open please.

(*The examination consists of examining eyes and mouth, feeling forehead, neck and underarm glands, joints of arms.*)

SURGEON. Are you healthy?

WINNIE. Eh? (*She realizes.*) Oh. Yeh.

CHARLOTTE. Sound 'er chest then.

SURGEON. It's not necessary.

CHARLOTTE. She might be bronchitic.

SURGEON. She isn't. (*He goes on to PITTY.*) Open please.

CHARLOTTE. That all it is?

WINNIE. Disappointed?

CHARLOTTE. Whass 'e testin' for, common cold?

SURGEON. Sergeant, shut that woman up please.

CHARLOTTE. En 'e lovely when 'e's strict!

SARGE. Button it!

CHARLOTTE. I'll stitch it up fer sixpence.

(*They laugh.*)

SARAH. What 'appens if yer find somethin' wrong, doctor?

SURGEON. You don't go.

CHARLOTTE. She don' wan' a go. (*She indicates PITTY.*)

SURGEON. (*To PITTY.*) Open your shirt please.

(*PITTY, scared, rigid, doesn't move.*)

CHARLOTTE. Oi, favouritism!

WINNIE. I didn't get that.

SURGEON. It's for your own good.

(*PITTY undoes her shirt.*)

SURGEON. Breathe in deeply. Out. That's it. (*He sounds her chest.*) Do your shirt up. Open your mouth again. (*He sticks a thermometer in it and goes on to MADGE.*)

WINNIE. You our ship's doctor?

SURGEON. No.

WINNIE. 'Oo is then?

SURGEON. I don't know. I've only been asked to carry out the pre-voyage examination.

SARAH. We got a doctor?

SURGEON. I don't think so.

CHARLOTTE. Would you come if they asked yer?

SURGEON. They didn't ask me.

WINNIE. Why en't yer comin' then?

SARGE. Let the man do 'is job, girls.

CHARLOTTE. Do it 'ere any time.

MADGE. Why en't yer comin'?

SURGEON. (*To MADGE.*) How old are you?

MADGE. Forty-three.

SURGEON. Healthy?

MADGE. Yes.

SURGEON. (*Moves on to NANCE.*) Open please.

NANCE. They asked you a question.

SURGEON. Open please.

NANCE. Why en't yer comin'?

SURGEON. If you must know, it's because these aren't convict-ships, they're warships. The Government declared war on rebellion in America and its bursting jails by investing in a new colony of thieves—not all of them in chains. After all, no one strands himself six months from civilization without a fight or a bribe. So aggression becomes profit and the war spreads. You're being pushed; your ship's captains, guards, and surgeons are being paid. And so the war goes on. The captains hurrying their cargoes to collect their fees; the guards bullying the cargoes into order; the surgeons botching them into health. You— the cargoes—rebel and are confined, flogged and starved for your trouble. The surgeon patches. Caught in the crossfire of a war without reason you can't expect humanity. It's also underpaid and I'm a poor sailor (*He takes the thermometer from PITTY's mouth, looks at it, then returns to NANCE.*) Open please.

(*NANCE opens.*)

CHARLOTTE. Why yer doin' this then?

SURGEON. One seriously sick person aboard a ship before it sails can mean heavy mortalities during the voyage. They also agreed my fee.

NANCE. What we doin' for a doctor then?

SURGEON. There's a small cupboard in the crew's quarters with a large red cross on it. If your captain finds no one between now and the time you sail, that will be your doctor. (*He moves on to CHARLOTTE.*) Open please.

CHARLOTTE. My legs or me shirt?

SURGEON. Open please. (*He examines CHARLOTTE.*)

SARAH. We got a 'ave a doctor though!

SURGEON. It's not insisted on.

WINNIE. Makes yer sick.

SURGEON. Are you healthy?

CHARLOTTE. Why, you got somethin' in mind?

SURGEON. Answer me.

CHARLOTTE. What do you think?

SURGEON. (*Moves on to SARAH.*) Open please.

CHARLOTTE. That all I get?

WINNIE. What about 'er? (*She indicates PITTY.*)

SURGEON. She's sound enough physically.

NANCE. An' what else?

SURGEON. (*To SARAH.*) Open your shirt please.

(*SARAH does so.*)

SURGEON. Breathe deeply. In. Out. (*He sounds her chest.*) Thank you. Are you healthy?

SARAH. Yes.

SURGEON. Sergeant.

(*SARGE opens the door. The two men go.*)

WINNIE. I could go for 'im.

CHARLOTTE. All 'e says is 'Open please.'

WINNIE. What more d'yer need?

CHARLOTTE. Only asked the pretty one t'open their shirts, didn't 'e.

WINNIE. Nothin' wrong with your chest. See that a mile off.

CHARLOTTE. Fuckin' oglin' Sarah, 'e was.

WINNIE. I bet 'e's seen 'undreds though.

ABIGAIL. Ain't killed 'is appetite, 'as it.

WINNIE. Just' gettin' selective in 'is old age.

SARAH. 'Er bust's better'n mine.

CHARLOTTE. He didn't think so, did 'e.

NANCE. It's only the sick 'e's after. You're strong as a bleedin' ox.

CHARLOTTE. 'Oo you callin' names? (*Pause.*) I'm bored already.

NANCE. Should a brought yer knittin'.

CHARLOTTE. I'll do you!

WINNIE. Cards? (*She holds a pack up.*)

SARAH. Where'd they come from?

CHARLOTTE. Up 'er knickers, where else.

WINNIE. What yer wan' a play?

CHARLOTTE. Can't get over there.

WINNIE. Both on full stretch?

(*WINNIE, SARAH and CHARLOTTE move as near the centre as their chains will let them.*)

WINNIE. (*To NANCE.*) You in?

NANCE. Why not. (*She joins them.*)

MADGE. Watch'er, she's a sharp.

WINNIE. Ah, what yer wan' a tell 'em for?

MADGE. Give us the pack.

(*NANCE snatches the pack and throws it to MADGE, who examines it expertly. WINNIE gropes in her drawers and pulls out another pack.*)

WINNIE. 'Ere's the marked ones.

MADGE.   Straight.   (*She gives the pack to CHARLOTTE.*)

WINNIE. What I tell yer? (*She holds out her hand to CHARLOTTE to take the cards back.*) Watch 'er deal.

CHARLOTTE. (*Holding on to the cards.*) Still warm!

WINNIE. What we playin'?

CHARLOTTE. Loo?

WINNIE. Right. Cut fer dealer. What we playin' for?

CHARLOTTE. What we got? (*She cuts.*)

WINNIE. Food? (*She cuts.*)

NANCE. Not food. Never. (*She cuts.*)

WINNIE. I deal. Points then. Think a somethin' later. (*She deals.*)

NANCE. So you're a sharper, are yer?

WINNIE. Whass this? Truth time?

CHARLOTTE. Why not.

WINNIE. Well then. I done a bit a most things really. Sharpin', pickpocketin', shopliftin'. Fam'ly business, see. Only the better-paid lines, mind. We like t'keep ourselves nice. Me an' me Mum got seven years apiece. Furniture under false pretenses.

SARAH. Furniture!?

WINNIE. 'Ad it delivered t' this empty 'ouse we knew.

SARAH. What for though?

WINNIE. We used t'run this weekly auction.

CHARLOTTE. Ever try the game?

WINNIE. Fer losers, en it. Diminishin' returns. You're at a disadvantage from the start, count a there's always a bloke in it. 'E's usually on top an' you're underneath. You're doin' it fer 'im. Specially if 'e's livin' off yer an' all. Then 'e walks out, yer got a worn-out fanny an' nothin' t' show fer it. 'Cept probably a kid. One thing I'm thankful t'my ol' man for, useless bastard. Never let us in fer that kind of crap.

CHARLOTTE. Do without, can yer?

WINNIE. Normally sexed, I am.

CHARLOTTE. Once every seven years. With 'er new skin.

MADGE. Thass what 'appened with this one. (*PITTY.*) Ran away from 'ome, from 'er parents in the country. Pregnant a course. 'Er fella goes with 'er, says 'e'll marry 'er. Keeps 'er a month then walks out. She miscarries, buggered every way she turns. Can't go 'ome. No trade. When 'er money runs out she's on the game. Total incompetent. First day out she gets picked up.

WINNIE. Didn't think they sent first offenders.

MADGE. She weren't. But when they let 'er out she weren't no wiser. She did it again, got caught again. Consequence is, she's still no wiser.

WINNIE. Whass your game, Nance?

NANCE. No game. I was 'onest, more or less. Used t'work, makin' shirts. Thought crime was fer mugs. Turns out politics is no better. I got fourteen years fer bashin' a peeler's 'ead with this lead pipin'. Went with me bloke up Kennin'ton Common. T' this meetin'. We took the lead, case a trouble. There was this group a fellas, 'ecklin' an' pushin'. They start fightin' my bloke's mates, so Johnnie Law comes stridin' in, truncheon swingin'. Fetches my bloke one on the ear'ole. 'E weren't doin' nothin', 'cept listen t' the speaker. Soon as 'e's down, they start carryin' 'im off. 'E give me the lead t' protec' meself, so I give the peeler what for. Then this other peeler grabs me an' I'm bashin' 'is shins, so they carry me off an' all. Plumber my bloke was. Thass 'ow 'e got the lead.

WINNIE. Whass 'e doin' now?

NANCE. Fourteen year, same as me. On the Duke a Portlan'. Doin' us a favor if we meet up again. Never fancied this rotten 'ole anyway. No chance fer an 'onest worker in this country, m'dears.

WINNIE. I 'eard if you're good over there they let yer go after a couple a years.

NANCE. 'Ow good though? Better'n them? Get nowhere fast that way.

WINNIE. Class pickpocket, this one. (*She indicates CHARLOTTE.*)

CHARLOTTE. Thass right.

MADGE. If yer're that good, clevertits, 'ow'd yer get caught?

CHARLOTTE. Put-up job weren't it. What yer get fer 'avin' a reputation. Seven years apiece, me an' Sarah. Picked us up on a bus. I'd jus' loosened this woman's purse when these four peelers get out their seats an' pounce on us. Yer don't get four plain clothes on a bus t'gether less they're tipped off. I was done all right too. Ten t' fifteen a week, wardrobe full a dresses. Restaurants.

SARAH. Workin' the classy areas, see. Racetracks, theatres. Real ladies.

CHARLOTTE. Yer got a look good, see. Know yer manners. Keep yer 'ands right. No washin' or scrubbin'. Short, neat nails. Fingers soft and supple. Not greasy, not dry. Competition grassed, I reckon.

SARAH. I'm fed up with this game.

WINNIE. Thass cos yer're losin'.

NANCE. What were you before that, Sarah? Dollymop?

SARAH. In service.

NANCE. What I tell yer!

SARAH. Only I didn't 'ang aroun' with no soldiers.

MADGE. Jus' villains.

SARAH. My bloke was all right. Clerk 'e was. Clean-livin'. Faithful. Bit bent, thass all. Didn't do me no good though. I chucked me job t'live with 'im an' 'e got done fer forgin'. I 'adn't bothered with references, I got involved in 'is trial, so I 'ad t' go on the game. Till Charlotte said 'er lark was better. Looks it now, don't it.

NANCE. Nothin' like gettin' nicked t'gether fer cementin' true love.

CHARLOTTE. Look in the corner if true love's what yer're after.

(*She indicates PITTY, who is curled up in MADGE's lap with a rag doll.*)

WINNIE. She's got a dolly!

CHARLOTTE. 'Ow's that fer mother-instinct.

MADGE. I tell yer it's a crime she's on this ship. She won't make the journey less we all look after 'er.

CHARLOTTE. We ain' all got your int'rest.

MADGE. Kill 'er, would yer?

CHARLOTTE. What were you anyway? A jealous madame?

MADGE. They give me seven year fer runnin' an employment agency.

NANCE. Bitch.

MADGE. They're the mugs. It's their look-out.

SARAH. Whass wrong with givin' people jobs?

NANCE. Yer don't. Thass the point. Yer put an 'ad in the papers askin' folk five bob t' find 'em a job. They send it in, then you make off with it.

SARAH. Neat.

MADGE. Would a been, 'cept me partner got caught collectin' the letters. Split on me, the cow.

NANCE. Serves yer right. Cheatin' them as needs it most.

MADGE. I been bilked enough by christian neighbours not t' love their charity, darlin'.

NANCE. That ain' charity fer our kind, it's common sense.

MADGE. If yer're soft.

NANCE. Whass that then? (*She indicates PITTY.*)

MADGE. Mutual advantage.

NANCE. Thass what I'm sayin'.

MADGE. It's not the same.

WINNIE. (*To NANCE.*) You playin' or not? I'm nearly out.

NANCE. (*Looks at her cards then throws them in.*) Fuckin' sharp.

WINNIE. (*Laying out her winning hand.*) Come six months yer might be takin' the odd game off me.

CHARLOTTE. Fuck that.

(*She throws in her hand. TOMMY appears outside the cell.*)

SARAH. 'Ere, look what's on 'im!

CHARLOTTE. Nothin' special. Seen that before.

NANCE. She means the food.

(*TOMMY is trying to balance three pots of food and a pile of eating utensils while unlocking the door at the same time.*)

NANCE. Whass 'e got?

TOMMY. Beef. Cabbage. Potatoes.

WINNIE. Smells all right.

CHARLOTTE. 'Urry up!

TOMMY. Give us a chance.

NANCE. Thass good food.

WINNIE. Better'n in nick.

CHARLOTTE. Whass fer afters?

TOMMY. Tea. I bring that after.

CHARLOTTE. When else.
NANCE. Get a move on!
TOMMY. I'll 'ave t' put somethin' down.

(*TOMMY puts the pots down and opens the door. They are all, except PITTY and MADGE, on taut chains as near the door as possible. TOMMY hesitates at the door.*)

TOMMY. I'll serv it 'ere.
CHARLOTTE. Cunt.
TOMMY. After yer've used 'em, these plates are yours. Wash 'em up in the bucket. I change it once a day.
CHARLOTTE. Come on.
TOMMY. This is your'n then.
CHARLOTTE. Good. (*She takes her food.*)
WINNIE. They got a make sure we're well-fed before we go. A week out a Falmouth, there'll be no more a this. Biscuits an' pease-pudden it'll be then. Ta. (*She takes her food.*)
CHARLOTTE. Whass your name again?
TOMMY. Tommy.
CHARLOTTE. 'Ow old are yer?
TOMMY. Sixteen.
CHARLOTTE. 'Oo d'yer fancy?
WINNIE. 'E's blushin' again!

(*TOMMY gives SARAH her plate. She smiles. He smiles.*)

WINNIE. Aye-aye! D'yer see that?
CHARLOTTE. Say n'more.
NANCE. Favoritism. 'Ow many spud 'e give yer, Sarah?
SARAH. Same as the others.
NANCE. Bit more greens, sonny.

TOMMY. You got the same.

NANCE. I'm bigger though.

MADGE. Yer're only takin' it from someone else.

NANCE. The Captain, thass all. Pile it on, son.

TOMMY. 'Ere are. (*He gives her the plate.*)

NANCE. (*Examines it.*) Let yer off this time.

TOMMY. (*To MADGE.*) You got two plates?

MADGE. For 'er. (*She indicates PITTY.*)

TOMMY. Whass wrong with 'er?

MADGE. She don' wan' a go, thass all.

TOMMY. I reckon it'll be interestin'.

NANCE. 'Oo's side you on, sonny?

TOMMY. It's my first time at sea.

CHARLOTTE. Don't believe in 'alf-measures, do yer.

(*TOMMY passes MADGE a plate. She puts it by PITTY. PITTY shows no interest.*)

NANCE. 'Cept with the food.

TOMMY. I give you the same.

NANCE. It's not enough though. Tell the Captain.

TOMMY. They said 'ow much t'give yer.

NANCE. Go back an' say I want more then.

TOMMY. It's me first day!

NANCE. Yer'll get in trouble if yer don't look after us.

TOMMY. If I ask fer more I will.

NANCE. You an' us both, son. Story a our lives.

SARAH. Leave 'im alone, Nance.

NANCE. 'Ark at love's young dream! Concentrate on whass important, darlin'.

(*She steals one of SARAH's potatoes.*)

SARAH. 'Ere!

TOMMY. You can't do that!

NANCE. First one comes near, I'll ram this in 'er face.

(*She retreats to her corner and brandishes her fork.*)

WINNIE. I'm eatin'.

CHARLOTTE. First chance I get, Nance, I'll knock your ears off.

NANCE. Everyone knows lovers don't get 'ungry.

TOMMY. 'Ere are.

(*He hands MADGE her second plate. NANCE sneaks another potato from it. MADGE kicks her shins.*)

NANCE. Whass the matter with you? She don' wan' it!

MADGE. Yer can always ask.

TOMMY. I ought t' report 'er.

WINNIE. You report 'er, I'll say yer tried t' rape 'er.

NANCE. Thass right. I got the bruises.

MADGE. We'll sort it out, son.

TOMMY. I'm gettin' the tea. (*He goes.*)

CHARLOTTE. (*To NANCE.*) 'Ave t' watch you, won't we.

NANCE. And you. You're the cut-purse around 'ere. 'Ang on t' yer bags t'night, girls.

CHARLOTTE. Got a fortune stashed away, 'ave yer?

NANCE. 'Ave you?

CHARLOTTE. I wou'nt tell you if I 'ad.

NANCE. 'Ere we go.

CHARLOTTE. Whass that s'possed t' mean?

NANCE. I ain' been in this tub 'alf an 'our, I'm sick a the soun' a your voice already. Shootin' yer mouth off, bitchin' all the time. Yer don't know when t' stop.

CHARLOTTE. So?

NANCE. Yer need a fuckin' gag on.

CHARLOTTE. You goin' a put it there?

NANCE. Thass not the point. This is the point. (*She holds a potato up on her fork.*) Nothin' else matters.

CHARLOTTE. Yer don't steal people's food.

NANCE. Why not?

CHARLOTTE. Think you're better do you?

NANCE. No. An' fer the same reason you don't go tellin' people what t' do.

CHARLOTTE. Whass that if it ain't an order?

NANCE. Know it all, don't yer.

CHARLOTTE. You said it.

(*TOMMY returns with the tea. He carries a bag of tea, lemon juice, sugar, six mugs and spoons.*)

NANCE. Stop stirrin' it is what I said.

CHARLOTTE. What's stirrin' it if that ain't?

NANCE. There's no 'ope in 'ere less we stick together.

CHARLOTTE. Potato-stealin' Radical we got 'ere. Go tell that up Kennin'ton Common.

NANCE. I'm jus' statin' the obvious.

CHARLOTTE. Not arf.

NANCE. Keep the air sweet.

CHARLOTTE. It's you that's gettin' steamed up.

NANCE. An' you that's playin' games. This ain' games. (*The potato.*)

CHARLOTTE. The air ain't sweet anyway. There ain't enough t' go roun'. We ain't t' fuckin' gether.

NANCE. There are.

(*She holds the potato out on her fork. CHARLOTTE takes it and gives it to SARAH.*)

NANCE. That one's 'ers. (*She indicates PITTY.*)

CHARLOTTE. Now 'oo's playin' games?

NANCE. I ain' competin'.

(*She gives the other potato to MADGE.*)

CHARLOTTE. Jus' chickenin' out.

NANCE. You set yerself up, girl, I'll knock yer down.

CHARLOTTE. I'd like t' see it.

NANCE. You will.

CHARLOTTE. Soon as these are off, I'll 'ave yer eyes out.

NANCE. I'll be ready for yer.

MADGE. An' me.

CHARLOTTE. So? Jus' means there's two a yer.

MADGE. Come on, Kathleen, eat up.

WINNIE. I'll 'ave it if she don't wan' it.

PITTY. Pigs!

WINNIE. Good on yer, girl.

TOMMY. 'Ere are, yer do this yerselves. Yer got a stove. There's water in the kettle an' yer keep the tea. Make it when yer like. It's got a last a week.

WINNIE. What, that little bit?

TOMMY. Thass not bad. 'Oo's goin' a be Mum?

WINNIE. Me.

TOMMY. That makes you Matron then. From now on you collect an' supervise the distribution a provisions. Yer're also responsible for the tidiness an' cleanliness a the cell.

WINNIE. All that jus' fer makin' a cup a tea?

NANCE. 'E's pulled 'is first fast one, en't yer, Tommy.

TOMMY. They told me t' do it that way. Else no-one'd volunteer, they said.

WINNIE. They were right an' all.

NANCE. Call us Ma'am in future when yer talk to us.

TOMMY. Yes, Ma'am.

(*The others laugh.*)

SARAH. Leave 'im alone, Nance.
TOMMY. Thass t' clean yer plates with, Ma'am. (*He throws a cloth in NANCE's face and goes to go.*)

NANCE. Charmin'!
SARAH. Serves yer right.
WINNIE. 'Ere, Tommy, yer dropped this.

(*She holds up a knife. TOMMY clutches his empty sheaf. He takes the knife from WINNIE and goes.*)

CHARLOTTE. What yer give it 'im for? I'ad that.
WINNIE. An' I saw yer.
CHARLOTTE. Could a been useful.
WINNIE. 'E's only young though.
NANCE. (*To CHARLOTTE.*) Good, en't she. (*She means WINNIE.*)
CHARLOTTE. Better be good at tea an' all.
SARAH. Yeh, come on, Matron, get weavin'.
WINNIE. Fuckin' 'ome from 'ome this is. One thing about prison food on land, least yer get service.
SARAH. What 'appens at night?
CHARLOTTE. 'E comes down an' screws yer.
SARAH. I was 'opin' yer'd say that.

(*They sway involuntarily.*)

WINNIE. 'Ere, it's rockin'. We ain' off, are we?
MADGE. It's the swell in the 'arbour.
NANCE. Whass the name a this tub anyway?
WINNIE. Sydney Cove.
SARAH. 'Oo's 'e when 'e's ome?
CHARLOTTE. Thass where we're goin', thickie.

SARAH. Oh.

Scene 4

Above the cell. A barrel.
SARGE and TOMMY, relaxing.

SARGE. Keep 'em 'appy at this stage, see son. Bring 'em on late. Give 'em a medical so they feel looked after. Feed 'em, then leave 'em. That way we get a decent night's sleep.

TOMMY. I see.

SARGE. The last we'll get, probably.

TOMMY. Oh?

SARGE. You ain' seen nothin' yet.

TOMMY. No?

SARGE. Women's ships are the worst, believe me. Yer might think women are soft, but once they sunk this low, they're like wild animals. Ain't got the control of a man, see. Tigresses when they get goin'. Get a real deliquent, there's no 'oldin' 'er. You can shave 'er 'ead, flog 'er back, lock 'er in a box, she won't be tamed.

TOMMY. Not surprisin' really.

SARGE. What d'yer mean?

TOMMY. I 'ad a bitch at 'ome once. Best way t' train 'er was bribin'. Bits a biscuit. If yer clouted 'er she got sulky. Why shou'n't she.

SARGE. Don't ask why, son. It's an aggressive question in these circumstances. They ain' logical creatures at the best a times. An' these ain' exactly intellectuals. Yer got a be on yer guard all the time.

TOMMY. I foun' that out.

SARGE. Why, what 'appened?

TOMMY. One of 'em 'ad me knife away.

SARGE. Yer got it back, I 'ope.

TOMMY. Only cos another of 'em stole it back an' give it me.

SARGE. It's like I said, see. No logic.

TOMMY. 'Ad a flamin' great row while I was in there too.

SARGE. Thass why it's good t' 'ave a Matron, see. Keep 'em in line. Soon sorts that ol' nonsense out of 'em. Natural 'aters of authority they are. But when they're sorted properly, see, organized with a Matron, settled in, responsible for their own actions—character shows. Yer see 'oo's cooperative, 'oo's cantakerous, a randy little 'ore, a col' fish. Then yer pick 'em off.

TOMMY. What for?

SARGE. Screwin', punishment, whatever yer fancy. They got a see 'oo's boss or our lives is misery.

TOMMY. Why d'you do this, Sarge?

SARGE. I told yer before, son, why's an aggressive question.

TOMMY. Sorry.

SARGE. (*Pause.*) It's what yer get out of it, en it. We're all on the make. Captain, Surgeon, Purser, First Mate. They make more'n me a course, but I ain' got their responsibility. We're all free in our different ways. They give me orders, but I'm still givin' more'n I'm takin'. I got used t' that in the army, see, an' this ain' so dangerous. Important to consider when yer get t' my age, see. Slowin' up. Then there's the perks. Women. Liquor, I'm 'appy enough, though. Foun' me level.

TOMMY. Don't yer get lonely?

SARGE. What d'yer mean?

TOMMY. Sort a 'ollow feelin'?

SARGE. Miss yer Mum, do yer?

TOMMY. It's not that.

SARGE. This is better'n all that, en it. Wife, kids, mother-in-law, fam'ly.

TOMMY. Thass what I thought.

SARGE. Anyway plen'y a women on this ship.

TOMMY. What, to 'ave?

SARGE. Sort out what yer fancy, it's as good as it lasts.

TOMMY. Oh.

SARGE. Seen anythin' yet?

TOMMY. I don't know. They all seem the same.

SARGE. Thass cos they all been through the same. They won't stay that way. Character shows. You'll see. Wan' some a this?

TOMMY. What is it?

SARGE. Rum. It's their ration. We got our own, but keep their measures down a touch, we get some t' relax with. 'Ave a go. (*He pours TOMMY a drink.*) 'Elps yer sleep.

Scene 5

In the cell.

WINNIE, PITTY, SARAH, CHARLOTTE, NANCE and MADGE.

CHARLOTTE. Gettin' a dab 'and at that tea-makin', Win.

NANCE. About time. She's 'ad a week of it.

(*WINNIE sweeps the floor in determined silence.*)

PITTY. Whyn't we get no fresh veg today?

CHARLOTTE. Thass yer lot, sunshine. They're finished now.

PITTY. Fuck that.

CHARLOTTE. I like 'er when she's normal like that.

(*PITTY nestles down in MADGE's lap.*)

WINNIE. Call that normal?

SARAH. I'm goin' a puke again.

CHARLOTTE. D'you 'ave to?

SARAH. I can't 'elp it. It won't stay down.

CHARLOTTE. Give 'er the bucket, someone.

SARAH. Oh!

CHARLOTTE. Quick!

(*WINNIE gets the bucket. SARAH is sick throughout most of the rest of this scene.*)

NANCE. 'Ow long's this go on for?

MADGE. Till she gets 'er sea-legs.

CHARLOTTE. It's not legs she needs, it's a new stomach. She's puked 'er old one up.

MADGE. She'll get used to it.

NANCE. Thass no answer.

CHARLOTTE. It's weakenin' 'er. She looks like a bloody ghost.

NANCE. It's the smell I can't stand.

(*WINNIE is staring hard at NANCE.*)

CHARLOTTE. Well, misery?

WINNIE. Only opens 'er mouth t'bellyache.

NANCE. Least 'alf me dinner don't come pourin' out.

WINNIE. I didn't know bein' made Matron meant cow-towin' t' bitches like you.

NANCE. 'Ow could yer? Yer didn't ask.

WINNIE. Just as well, en it.

NANCE. Comes natural t' some.

WINNIE. Whass that s'posed t'mean?

NANCE. Yer're a born lackey, darlin'.

CHARLOTTE. We gotta listen to all that again?

NANCE. She walked right into it! All the slave's bloody jobs! If she ain' a natural she's a bleedin' madwoman.

WINNIE. I got better things t' do 'n listen to you.

NANCE. Like what? Sweep the floor?

WINNIE. Thass right.

NANCE. She's off 'er 'ead.

(*WINNIE sweeps assiduously.*)

NANCE. It ain' doin' yer no good, yer know. They ought a pay someone fer that.

CHARLOTTE. Shut up, will yer.

(*WINNIE sweeps.*)

NANCE. What d'you get out of it? Eh?

(*WINNIE sweeps.*)

NANCE. S'posin' I shit on the floor? You'd carry the can. With my shit in it.

WINNIE. I bloody wouldn't!

NANCE. You're nominally responsible fer this cell bein' cleanly an' efficiently run.

WINNIE. I'm also in charge.

CHARLOTTE. Whoa-hey!

WINNIE. I can report you if you give me trouble.

NANCE. Report me, darlin', I'll bust that broom on yer 'ead.

WINNIE. That won't do yer no good.

NANCE. Won' exactly be a tonic for you either. You ain' doin' yerself no good by this.

WINNIE. They might commute my sentence.

NANCE. They tell yer that?

WINNIE. 'Inted at it.

NANCE. Bitch! (*She spits on the floor.*) Sweep that up.

CHARLOTTE. Silly cow.

(*WINNIE ignores the spit. She sweeps round it.*)

NANCE. Believe that crap, you'll believe anythin'!

(*Pause. WINNIE finishes sweeping.*)

CHARLOTTE. (*To Sarah.*) 'Ow's it goin', love?

SARAH. When's it goin' a stop?

NANCE. Fuckin' marvellous, the pairin' off in 'ere. There's Madam Lesbos and the late Prime Minister in one corner, Elizabeth Fry an' the vomitin' soldier in the other, an' I'm stuck with labourin' 'Ercules 'ere. 'Oo shuffled this pack?

MADGE. Why don't yer shut up an' leave us in peace?

NANCE. I got a sleep next to it every night. It's criminal, three on a bed.

CHARLOTTE. There's always the floor.

NANCE. An' 'ave the rats crawlin' all over me? Quick midnight snack fer the cockroaches? I'm tryin' a exterminate the buggers, not bloody subsidize 'em.

(*SARGE and TOMMY appear.*)

CHARLOTTE. Look what the tide's brought in.

NANCE. All I need's the laughin' p'liceman.

SARGE. Enjoy yer first sailor's dinner, me darlin's.

CHARLOTTE. Got a be a sadist t'enjoy your job, en't yer.

SARGE. Don' roll those eyes at me, Charlotte. Once I'm encouraged there's no 'oldin' me.

CHARLOTTE. I'd 'ave t' be desperate t' encourage you. 'Ow'd d'yer know me name anyway?

SARGE. I got you marked out fer special treatment.

CHARLOTTE. I ain' seen none of it.

SARGE. In time, girl. We're 'ardly a week under sail

PITTY. Feels like six months.

SARGE. Nothin' like lookin' on the bright side, is there, sunshine. (*He stands by CHARLOTTE and strokes her hair.*) Now then. Official business. T'night's the first a my weekly inspections. I come t'make sure yer're all feelin' well an' keepin' yerselves clean an' orderly.

CHARLOTTE. So what yer doin' wi' me 'air? Checkin' fer nits?

SARGE. Yer never know.

CHARLOTTE. (*Pulling away.*) Keep yer bleedin' 'ands t' yourself then!

SARGE. (*Kneeling beside her.*) There are all kinds a privilege on convict ships, Charlotte. Mostly kept fer the favored few.

CHARLOTTE. I like your cheek!

SARGE. Long as I'm appreciated.

CHARLOTTE. Touch me again, I'll bust these chains on yer 'ead.

SARGE. Every curse a kiss. I shall treasure 'em all.

TOMMY. Whass wrong with 'er? (*SARAH.*)

MADGE. Need you ask?

NANCE. She's been seasick since we left. Your weekly inspection's come none too soon, sergeant. Another day an' she'd puke 'er 'eart up.

TOMMY. You all right, Miss?

SARAH. Oh! (*She grabs hold of TOMMY.*)

SARGE. Yer're well away there, son. It's nothin' t' worry about, ladies. Quite normal. I'm surprised there ain't more a yer.

WINNIE. We were all sick first day out. 'Cept 'er. (*MADGE.*)

SARGE. Well-seasoned, eh.

MADGE. I'll see you in the grave, Gran'pa.

SARGE. Don't kid yerself, bag.

MADGE. I could give you ten years.

SARGE. Five at the outside.

CHARLOTTE. Whyn't you two get t'gether an' discuss the Norman invasion?

SARGE. I don't think I'm 'er type.

TOMMY. This one ought t' see the surgeon, Sarge.

NANCE. Where's a surgeon come from all of a sudden?

WINNIE. One 'oo give us the medical said 'e weren't comin'.

SARGE. Captain appealed to 'is better side. Right 'and back trouser. Where 'is wallet is.

CHARLOTTE. Whyn't 'e been roun' then?

SARGE. Incapacitated 'isself, I'm afraid. Bad touch a the bottle. Says 'e can never face the first few days. Pukin' like a dog. Why 'e's in the business I don't know. 'E's up today though.

TOMMY. I'll get 'im, shall I?

SARGE. One in number seventeen, tell 'im.

(*TOMMY rushes off.*)

SARGE. Take yer time.

(*TOMMY slows down. SARGE sees the spit on the floor.*)

SARGE. Whass this?

NANCE. Whass it look like?

SARGE. 'Oo's is it?

NANCE. Mine.

SARGE. You got spit on your floor, Matron.

WINNIE. She did it delib'rate.

SARGE. Did she now?

WINNIE. T'goad me.

SARGE. (*To NANCE.*) Don't like takin' orders, eh?

WINNIE. She's all right.

SARGE. Not if she spits on the floor she ain't. You goin' a report 'er?

WINNIE. What for?

SARGE. Provocation. Deliberate.

WINNIE. She spit, thass all. She knew I'd 'ave t' clear it up.

SARGE. You ain't though, it's my weekly inspection, there's spit on the floor an' you're responsible for it.

WINNIE. No I ain', she is.

SARGE. YOU'RE IN CHARGE.

WINNIE. Oh.

NANCE. You report me, Win, I'll do you good an' proper. I just about 'ad enough a this Matron crap.

SARGE. Intimidation now, is it?

NANCE. Look, don' come that with me, short arse. I know what you're up to, even if she don't. Either yer flog me or yer piss off out of it

SARGE. D'you 'ear that, Matron?

WINNIE. Yes, sergeant.

SARGE. Is that a way t' talk about yer senior jailer?

WINNIE. I don't know.

SARGE. You ought a report 'er to me. Otherwise any benefits as might accrue from your office could be wiped out.

SARGE. (*Pause.*) Yer don' wan' a black mark, do yer?

WINNIE. (*Quiet.*) No.

SARGE. Well then?

WINNIE. (*Quiet.*) She spat on my floor, Sarge.

SARGE. What yer say?

WINNIE. (*Firm.*) She spat on my floor.

(*NANCE leaps up and goes to strike WINNIE with the broom. SARGE intervenes and gets kicked on the shins. He wrenches the broom away and beats NANCE with it. When he's finished:*)

SARGE. An incident, ladies. Thass' ow we deal with incidents.

(*TOMMY comes back. NANCE stirs.*)

SARGE. Stay here!

(*NANCE does.*)

SARGE. Now listen. In the int'rest of 'ealth an' 'ygiene, an' against my better judgement an' experience, the Surgeon 'as persuaded the Captain that as from today prisoners will be allowed t' wander unchained in their cells. Tommy. (*He throws TOMMY a key with which the boy unlocks the prisoners' chains.*) This is not an invitation t'run riot, you understand, but a 'umane gesture t' keep yer blood circulatin' an' yer limbs exercised. In the circumstances it's as well we've weeded out in advance the inevitable element likely to abuse the privilege.

MADGE. You provoked 'er, fat-gut.

SARGE. Difficult t' prove in a court a law, Gran'ma.

(*CHARLOTTE, freed, gets up and kicks NANCE.*)

MADGE. Watch out!

(*NANCE tries to retaliate, CHARLOTTE kicks her again.*)

NANCE. Uch. (*She gives up.*)
MADGE. Not when she's down, girl!
CHARLOTTE. I can't 'elp 'er troubles. She bent the rules first. I been waitin' fer that.
MADGE. What about chainin' 'er up? (*CHARLOTTE.*)
SARGE. 'Igh spirits, thass all. I dare say she 'ad 'er reasons. (*He gropes CHARLOTTE.*)
CHARLOTTE. Leave my bum alone.
SARGE. Give us an 'and, son.

(*They thread the broom through NANCE's chains and carry her off like a hunted wild animal.*)

WINNIE. Cow.
CHARLOTTE. Changed yer tune, 'ave yer?
WINNIE. You got a yella streak six miles wide.
CHARLOTTE. She 'ad 'er warnin'. Nothin' worse'n stealin' food, I knew 'e wou'nt touch me.
MADGE. Got 'im nicely sorted, en't yer.
CHARLOTTE. 'E thinks 'e's got me sorted, so it's fair. Anyway, it weren't me landed the poor cow in it. She ought a be shot.
WINNIE. What could I do? 'E made me responsible!
MADGE. Once 'e's got you workin' for 'im, we're all under 'is thumb. Tell 'im where t' get off. We'll back yer up.
WINNIE. What about gettin' me sentence commuted?

MADGE. Got the power to, 'as 'e?

WINNIE. I don't know.

MADGE. D'yer trust 'im?

WINNIE. No.

MADGE. Well then. Yer got six months doin' everythin' 'e says, not knowin' if 'e'll keep 'is side a the bargain. One slip an' yer're done fer. Livin' with us 'oo won' love yer fer it. Against that yer trust us t' stick by yer.

WINNIE. Nance won't, not now.

MADGE. Thass what she lives by, en it, us versus them. She'll only 'ound yer if yer stay Matron. Stick with us, she's got no quarrel with yer.

(*SURGEON appears.*)

WINNIE. Yeh well.

MADGE. You'll see.

SURGEON. (*Coming in.*) Who's sick?

CHARLOTTE. She is.

SURGEON. Give her this. (*He throws her a bottle of medicine.*)

CHARLOTTE. Whass this?

(*SURGEON goes to go.*)

CHARLOTTE. Oi you! She needs proper treatment. A bed to 'erself, warm clothin'. She's kep' nothin' down fer a week!

SURGEON. I've been through half the ship. There are nineteen in her condition. Including myself. None of us can have beds. I need them for the diseased.

CHARLOTTE. You can get 'er another blanket, can't yer?

SURGEON. There are none to spare.

SARAH. 'Ow long's it goin' a last, doctor?
SURGEON. Probably not more than another week.
CHARLOTTE. I like your probably!
SURGEON. No-one else ill?
CHARLOTTE. Thank yerself lucky.

(*SURGEON goes.*)

CHARLOTTE. 'Ere, 'ow's she take it?
SURGEON. One spoonful after meals. I'll be back.
CHARLOTTE. They all say that, darlin'.
SURGEON. Tomorrow.
CHARLOTTE. You're welcome any time, lover.

(*SURGEON goes.*)

WINNIE. Fancy a quick 'and?
CHARLOTTE. I wou'nt mind 'is.
WINNIE. If yer lose, yer sweep the floor nex' week.
CHARLOTTE. Sod off.
WINNIE. I'll give meself an 'andicap.
CHARLOTTE. You're a pain, Winnie, you know that?
WINNIE. Four 'undred points.
CHARLOTTE. 'Ow about tyin' a scarf round yer eyes
an' cuttin' yer arms off:
WINNIE. Come on, thass generous!
CHARLOTTE. Get stuffed.
WINNIE. I'll let yer off the firs' time I'm supposed t'
report yer.
CHARLOTTE. You ain' reportin' no-one.
WINNIE. Firs' whack at surgeon.
CHARLOTTE. I already got that. You got nothin' t'
bargain with, Winnie.
WINNIE. (*To MADGE.*) Modest, en't she.

CHARLOTTE. Look, fuck off, Winnie, I don' wan' a know.—Sarah. Get this down yer.

(*She gives SARAH her medicine. SARGE and TOMMY arrive with NANCE, who has been put in a barrel, so only her arms and legs protrude.*)

WINNIE. Christ Almighty!

MADGE. Shut up.

WINNIE. What they done to 'er?

NANCE. (*As they come in.*) You done this as much as them!

MADGE. (*To SARGE.*) Cunt!

SARGE. Plenty more where that came from, Gran'ma.

NANCE. Shut yer mouth.

SARGE. You're not gettin' out a there till yer mend your manners. (*He goes with TOMMY.*)

NANCE. Cunt!

MADGE. Whass the idea a that?

NANCE. S'possed t' 'restrain' me. I told 'im no beer-barrel's ever 'ad that effect before. Soon as I apologize, 'e reckons, they'll let me out.

WINNIE. You ain' got a apologize t' me, Nance.

NANCE. I weren't goin' a.

CHARLOTTE. Looks like the Loch Ness bleedin' monster.

NANCE. You got somethin' comin' t' you!

CHARLOTTE. Latest from Paris, that is. All wearin' 'em down the Shomps-a-Leessays. Called the O-line. Specially designed fer embarrassed mothers-t'-be.

NANCE. Wan' a parade, do yer?

CHARLOTTE. Go on then.

(*Pause. Then, aggressively mimicking the poses of a mannequin, NANCE hobbles up and down. The others*) *laugh. CHARLOTTE begins singing. The others join in.)*

GIRLS.
LET US DRINK A GOOD HEALTH TO OUR
    SCHEMERS ABOVE
WHO AT LENGTH HAVE CONTRIVED FROM THIS
    LAND TO REMOVE
THESE ROBBERS AND VILLAINS, THEY'LL SEND
    US AWAY
TO BECOME A NEW PEOPLE IN BOTANY BAY.
SOME MEN SAY THEY HAVE TALENTS AND
    TRADES TO GET BREAD
BUT THEY SPONGE ON MANKIND TO BE CLOTHED
    AND FED
THEY'LL SPEND ALL THEY GET AND TURN NIGHT
    INTO DAY
NOW I'D HAVE ALL SUCH SOTS SENT TO BOTANY
    BAY.
    WINNIE. 'Ard on the knees, en it?
    NANCE. You shut up.
    CHARLOTTE. Can't see yer makin' the Palace in that.
    NANCE. 'Ere, give us me pipe

(MADGE goes to light it.)

    NANCE. No, 'er. The lackey. Light it for us.

(WINNIE lights her pipe.)

    NANCE. Thass not bad. I can smoke, dance, talk, eat. I could get t'Sydney an' not apologize.
    WINNIE. Yer don' 'ave to. We'll tell 'im yer did.
    NANCE. Not to you, to 'im! 'E wants t' see it fer 'isself. I'll collapse in a 'eap first.

CHARLOTTE. Not in that yer won't.
MADGE. Can yer sit down?

(*NANCE tries clumsily and fails.*)

MADGE. Thass the point of it, yer see. Yer can't sit down.
WINNIE. Crafty, en it.
NANCE. Shut up. (*She tries again and falls over. She rolls helplessly.*) Agh!

(*MADGE and WINNIE stop the barrel rolling.*)

WINNIE. You all right?
NANCE. That 'urt.
MADGE. We'll get you up.
NANCE. No 'ang on. Let's see. (*She tries to arrange herself comfortably in the barrel.*) 'Old it still. (*She goes through the motions of settling down to sleep.*) Can't sleep in it neither.
MADGE. It wears you out.
NANCE. 'Eavy an' all.
SARAH. Poor sod.
CHARLOTTE. You back with us?
SARAH. That stuff's not bad.
NANCE. Get us up then. I can't lie down 'ere for ever.
MADGE. Try the edge of the bed.

(*They help her to the bed. NANCE sits.*)

NANCE. Christ, get me up! It's killin' me!

(*They help her to her feet. Pause.*)

NANCE. Ingenious. What a cunt that man is.

CHARLOTTE. I'll sort 'im out.

NANCE. Not on yer own yer won't.

CHARLOTTE. You ain' goin' a 'elp much like that.

SARAH. Whyn't yer just apologize?

NANCE. Fuck off! If 'e thinks 'e can beat us that easy, 'e's got us by the fanny. I'd sooner collapse. Then the surgeon'll bawl 'im out.

SARAH. Be easier the other way.

WINNIE. Yer don' wan' a kill yerself jus' t' spite that bastard.

NANCE. I ain' goin' a kill meself an' it ain' just' fer that.

WINNIE. We're be'ind yer. Nance.

NANCE. Yeh, I noticed.

WINNIE. I ain' reportin' no-one no more. Stuff Matron.

(*NANCE looks at CHARLOTTE.*)

CHARLOTTE. It's your funeral, en it.

NANCE. (*Pause.*) I'll see 'ow it goes.

PITTY. We could take the weight off it for yer.

(*They all look round. PITTY has spoken.*)

NANCE. Only prolong it. Sooner I collapse the better. They'll take it off me then.

(*TOMMY is standing outside the door.*)

WINNIE. What do you want?

TOMMY. I'm off now.

WINNIE. Off where? Swimmin'?

TOMMY. Off duty. I'm sorry about that. (*The barrel.*)

NANCE. No good bein' sorry. Yer wan' a complain.

TOMMY. I told Sarge I didn't think it was right. 'E said t' keep me nose out of it.

NANCE. Next time shout down 'is ear'ole.

TOMMY. 'Ow's Sarah?

WINNIE. Thass what 'e's really down fer.

TOMMY. I jus' wondered.

WINNIE. Ask 'er.

TOMMY. Can I come in?

NANCE. You're the jailer.

(*TOMMY comes in. He looks at SARAH. She is still weak.*)

WINNIE. Ask 'ow she is then

TOMMY. 'Ow are yer, Sarah?

SARAH. Yer don' soun' very int'rested.

TOMMY. I'm embarrassed with them 'ere.

WINNIE. Leave the door open, we'll go.

SARAH. I'm better fer that med'cine. Don' know why I cou'nt 'ave it sooner, though.

NANCE. The surgeon's a cunt, that's why.

CHARLOTTE. You're talkin' about the man I love.

NANCE. 'Ard luck. I don' wan' 'im down 'ere at nights.

CHARLOTTE. You goin' a stop 'im?

TOMMY. What you talkin' about?

WINNIE. Visitors, love. We're drawin' up a list.

TOMMY. Oh.

CHARLOTTE. What yer lookin' sheepish for, yer silly cunt. Put yer arm roun' 'er.

TOMMY. Eh?

CHARLOTTE. Yer fancy 'er, don't yer?

TOMMY. Yeh, but.

WINNIE. What yer waitin' fer?

TOMMY. I don' know. (*To SARAH.*) Shall I?

SARAH. 'Bout time someone asked me!
TOMMY. Well?
SARAH. I'm not goin' a tell yer to!
TOMMY. I don't know if yer wan' me to.
WINNIE. Some people don' 'alf lead sheltered lives.
TOMMY. What yer think?
SARAH. Don' if yer don' wan' a!

(*TOMMY sits there. Pause. They all wait. Suddenly he puts his arm round SARAH.*)

WINNIE. I thought it was never comin'.

Scene 6

The cell in darkness. Everyone asleep.

NANCE is still in the barrel. The door opens and SARGE comes in. CHARLOTTE wakes up.

CHARLOTTE. 'Oo's that?
SARGE. Only me, darlin'.
CHARLOTTE. What do you want?
SARGE. Move over. (*He begins taking his boots off.*)
CHARLOTTE. What for?
SARGE. Come on, it's cold.
CHARLOTTE. There's four on 'ere already.

(*SARGE stops undressing.*)

SARGE. Four? (*He sees TOMMY asleep between CHARLOTTE and SARAH.*) 'Oo's that?
CHARLOTTE. 'Oo'd yer think?

SARGE. Deceptive, that lad. 'E knows it's against the rule, does 'e.

CHARLOTTE. What you doin' 'ere then?

SARGE. I can't sleep on me own. I feel the cold. (*He takes his trousers off.*)

CHARLOTTE. There's no room 'ere.

SARGE. We'll find some. You an' I. Now then. (*He tries to lie down with CHARLOTTE. She throws him off.*) Now come on, Charlotte, don't play around.

CHARLOTTE. 'Oo d'yer think you are?

SARGE. Yer know yer wan' it.

CHARLOTTE. I'm savin' meself.

SARGE. Be'ave like it too.

CHARLOTTE. Come an' find out then.

SARGE. Thass a girl. (*He joins CHARLOTTE on the bunk.*) Oh, thass better.

CHARLOTTE. Comfy?

SARGE. Very nice.

CHARLOTTE. Good.

SARGE. Uch.

(*CHARLOTTE has SARGE by the throat. She sits astride his stomach and bounces up and down on it during the following lines.*)

CHARLOTTE. Whass the idea, comin' in this time a night, disturbin' our sleep, eh? (*The others wake up.*) 'Oo gave you special right?

SARGE. Leggo!

CHARLOTTE. Think we're 'ere fer your convenience, do yer?

SARGE. Yer're chokin' me!

CHARLOTTE. Yer can't jus' walk in a' take what yer like, yer know!

SARGE. I'm warnin' you!

CHARLOTTE. 'Ave a bit a respect!

(*SARGE throws her off, rather more violently than he needs to.*)

WINNIE. 'Ere, whass your game?
CHARLOTTE. That does it. You've 'ad it now.

(*SARGE just has time to collect his boots and trousers before CHARLOTTE flies at him. He dodges her and reaches the door before she does. He locks it while she speaks.*)

CHARLOTTE. I told you you weren't welcome. I'm not that 'ard up for offers I got a put up with your kind. Yer can't beat 'ell out of us one day an' expect favors the next. RAPIST!

(*SARGE has gone.*)

SARAH. What'd 'e do?
CHARLOTTE. (*Getting back into bed.*) Comin' it.
SARAH. Oh. (*She goes back to sleep.*)
CHARLOTTE. No room fer four, let alone five.
NANCE. 'E's slep' right through it.
WINNIE. Check.
CHARLOTTE. Floatin' brothel it may be, but it's the inmates 'oo set the tone.
NANCE. Not always.
CHARLOTTE. Jus' cos you're out a action.
NANCE. Thanks.
CHARLOTTE. Nothin' to' do with you. (*Pause.*) Bloody nerve.

Scene 7

Above the cell.

SARGE, SURGEON and the CAPTAIN, behind his table.

SURGEON. I think we should stop.

CAPTAIN. I'm sorry. I'm being paid nine pound ten a head for these girls. With a hundred and three heads, that's nearly a thousand pounds. Over six months that's six pounds a day. Every day we're in Cape Town I lose six pounds.

SURGEON. If you lose a life, you lose more.

CAPTAIN. I'm prepared to take the risk.

SURGEON. If we stop we can take on fresh water, meat and vegetables. They can get in the sun and the fresh air.

CAPTAIN. And a week later we'll be in the same condition we're in now. Except a week further from Sydney.

SARGE. I think we should stop, sir.

CAPTAIN. So you can sell what you've creamed off the prisoners' supplies. I suppose.

SARGE. It'll do the men good, sir. They need t' unwind.

CAPTAIN. I hear them unwinding every night, sergeant. From my cabin, which God knows is far enough away from both their quarters and the women's.

SARGE. They get more difficult to control, thass all.

CAPTAIN. Are we short on anything?

SARGE. There won' be much spare by the time we get t' Sydney.

CAPTAIN. Lack of 'spare' depresses you does it sergeant.

SARGE. If we get 'eld up at all, sir.

CAPTAIN. We won't be.

SURGEON. I don't see how you can say that?

CAPTAIN. I know this ship!

SURGEON. Do you know the weather? The temperament of these women? His guard?

CAPTAIN. I've got no money for extra supplies. All we've got to trade with are tools, tackle and equipment. They need that in Sydney.

SARGE. They need everything in Sydney.

CAPTAIN. But not in Cape Town. The price is lower, and if I claim for reimbursement I won't see it till ten months from now, after the voyage home—which you two won't be on.

SURGEON. Disease doesn't spare anyone.

CAPTAIN. I've come through this far and I've been thirty years at sea.

SURGEON. Bad water begins it, confinement aggravates it, excessive physical punishment exacerbates it. Then it can reach anyone, particularly the weak. If we can't stop for supplies, I want an end to these ridiculous punishments.

CAPTAIN. The Sergeant knows his job.

SURGEON. It's in my contract.

CAPTAIN. What do you call 'excessive'?

SARGE. Before you go into that, gentlemen, I was thinkin' a little light industry might be beneficial. If the women were kept busy workin', they might be less boist'rous. We got cotton aboard. Cloth. Needles.

SURGEON. What price are shirts fetching in Sydney, Sergeant?

SARGE. More'n raw cloth, sir, I know that.

CAPTAIN. I'll divide the difference with the Guard fifty-fifty.

SARGE. Very fair, sir.

SURGEON. You're bartering with their health!

SARGE. Oh no, sir. It's all in the mind, en it.

Scene 8

WINNIE, SARAH, MADGE and PITTY are brought back to the cell by TOMMY.

WINNIE. Call that exercise?

TOMMY. Shut yer mouth.

SARAH. Don't talk to 'er like that.

TOMMY. All she does is belly-ache. It ain' my fault they didn't give yer long t'day. There's rough weather comin' up.

SARAH. So?

TOMMY. They wanted yer below. Safe. Out of it.

SARAH. Don't tell us though, do they. Jus' pushin' an' shoutin'.

TOMMY. They didn't wan' a frighten yer.

SARAH. Kids, are we?

TOMMY. Be'ave like it sometimes.

SARAH. Shou'nt be a jailer, should yer.

TOMMY. Thass all I am, is it.

SARAH. No fuckin' lover, I tell yer that much.

TOMMY. Plen'y a choice on this ship, yer know.

SARAH. Only if yer're a jailer.

TOMMY. I work fuckin' 'ard fer you lot, I don' 'ave t' do all I do. I don't get no thanks from the Captain neither.

WINNIE. Mister Bleedin' Wonderful, you are.

TOMMY. Thanks fer the sympathy. (*He goes out.*)

SARAH. We need more'n sympathy!

TOMMY. (*Outside.*) Well, you ain' gettin' no more favors. (*He goes.*)

WINNIE. I like that! We let 'im come down 'ere every night fer 'is bit of 'ole, put up with 'is gruntin' an' snortin', an' e's got the cheek t' talk about favors!

SARAH. I'm the one 'oo's doin' the favors.

WINNIE. Yer shou'nt a said what yer said about 'is lovin'. You enjoy it, don't yer?

SARAH. Get stuffed.

WINNIE. I wish I could, girl.

MADGE. (*Pause.*) Where'd Charlotte go?

SARAH. Library.

WINNIE. Maniac, she is with them bloody books.

SARAH. Doin' all right for 'erself though. Be educated by the time she gets off.

WINNIE. Readin' classes!

SARAH. Good luck t' 'er I say! Cou'nt make 'ead nor tail of it when I went.

PITTY. You're just thick.

SARAH. 'Ark at egg-head!

WINNIE. Not doin' us no good though, is it. Water still stinks. Still got the cockroaches.

SARAH. Nance goin' a smash 'em for yer? Pee in the water t' make it pure?

WINNIE. Nance is all right.

SARAH. If she is, we're all up shit creek.

PITTY. What'll they do to 'er this time?

SARAH. Cut 'er fanny out.

WINNIE. She's got some pluck though. Yer got a give it to 'er. Callin' the Captain a cunt in the middle a exercise, then slammin' Sarge in the teeth fer tryin' t' quiet 'er. It's the only way.

SARAH. They'll probably 'ang 'er for it too.

PITTY. She asked fer it, she'll get it.

WINNIE. I'm not sayin' she's clever, Pitty, I'm sayin' she gives 'em a run for their money.

MADGE. An' their money's what it's all about. If we'd stopped at the Cape we'd 'ave good water now.

PITTY. An' vegetables.

SARAH. An' less of everything else cos they'd a flogged off the surplus.

MADGE. They'll do that anyway in Sydney.

SARAH. Jus' prolongin' things.

WINNIE. On bad water. An' smelly fuckin' beddin'.

SARAH. Thass your fault fer not washin'.

WINNIE. In that? (*She points to the bucket.*)

SARAH. If yer're goin' a fight, at least you ought a know yer're goin' a win.

WINNIE. If they whip 'er, I'm puttin' in a complaint when we get t' Sydney.

SARAH. They won't love yer fer that.

WINNIE. Can't 'elp their troubles.

(*TOMMY brings CHARLOTTE back to the cell. She is holding on to his arm.*)

CHARLOTTE. Thank you, kind sir.

TOMMY. Piss off. (*He lets her go, then goes immediately.*)

CHARLOTTE. Whass wrong with 'im? Like that all the way from the library. Wou'nt speak t' me.

WINNIE. Don' love us no more.

SARAH. She was rude to 'im.

WINNIE. Love's young dream woke up suddenly, thass all.

MADGE. What yer get?

CHARLOTTE. "The Rise of Christianity in the Pagan World" by G.H. Farquhar.

MADGE. Not more religion?

CHARLOTTE. It was that or The Common Prayer Book again.

MADGE. En't they got no novels?

WINNIE. Not what they teach yer t'read for is it.

SARAH. I'd get bored.

CHARLOTTE. It's cos I'm bored I'm readin' the bloody things.

MADGE. I'll 'ave it after.

CHARLOTTE. Yer always wait fer me t' get 'em. Get one yerself, yer lazy cow.

WINNIE. Don't you share nothin'?

CHARLOTTE. Yeh, all the time. Since I been 'ere I've 'ad me comb nicked, me brooch an' me earrings.

WINNIE. Serves yer right fer 'avin' 'em.

CHARLOTTE. Wonderful not to, is it?

WINNIE. No good to anyone, are they.

CHARLOTTE. Why steal 'em then.

MADGE. Bring you down t' size?

CHARLOTTE. Very clever. Like what Nance did, I suppose.

PITTY. (*Pause.*) Madge is clever.

MADGE. Shut up.

PITTY. Madge can read.

MADGE. Sshh.

PITTY. Don't shush me. I'm not a little girl.

CHARLOTTE. Just a pain in the arse.

(*SARGE and TOMMY lead NANCE in. She has been flogged.*)

MADGE. Whass this?

WINNIE. What you done to 'er?

SARGE. Get that door open!

(*TOMMY opens the door. SARGE throws NANCE in. She falls.*)

NANCE. Cunt.

(*SARGE smashes her across the face.*)

NANCE. Oh!
WINNIE. 'Ere!
MADGE. Whass the idea?
SARGE. I'll shut you lot up if it kills me. Chain 'er up!

(*TOMMY does so.*)

SARGE. I wan' better'n this, Matron.
WINNIE. You got the wrong person.
SARGE. Charlotte?
CHARLOTTE. Go an' play with yerself.
SARGE. Solid be'ind the martyr, are we?
CHARLOTTE. Cheap 'eroics, thass all.
SARAH. No need to 'alf-kill 'er though.
PITTY. Whass 'e done to 'er?
SARGE. Twen'y-four lashes, sunshine. Unusual, but you lot got a learn. I lost two teeth on 'er account, an' thass not somethin' I take kindly to.
MADGE. They ought to string you up!
SARAH. (*To TOMMY.*) Jus' stood there an' watched, did yer?
TOMMY. I was down 'ere with you! I cou'nt do nothin'!
SARAH. Still chained 'er up though, didn't yer.
SARGE. Rate you're goin', sonny, you'll finish up in 'ere with 'em.

(*SARGE and TOMMY go.*)

NANCE. I thought 'e was a pal a yours.

CHARLOTTE. Thass not the only thing yer got wrong.

WINNIE. Anythin' yer want?

NANCE. Tea, love.

SARAH. What was it like, Nance?

NANCE. Fuck off.

PITTY. No!

MADGE. Whass the matter?

PITTY. Go away! I don't want you. I don't like you any more.

MADGE. Kathleen, they're all listenin'.

PITTY. Don't touch me!

MADGE. Kathleen, don't be silly.

PITTY. Go away! I don't want you. I don't like you any more.

WINNIE. Pitty, I'm makin' some tea.

PITTY. I don' wan' none.

MADGE. Calm done.

PITTY. You're dirty! I don' wan' a see you.

SARAH. Shut 'er up, can't yer?

MADGE. What d'yer think I am? A bloody zookeeper? I don't know what she wants.

CHARLOTTE. Ignore 'er.

WINNIE. Pitty, Nance's been whipped.

PITTY. She makes trouble. She deserves it.

WINNIE. Oh my God.

(*She advances on PITTY*)

PITTY. I get whipped every day. I'll show you the marks.

WINNIE. (*Stopping.*) Stop 'er, somebody.

(*No one moves.*)

WINNIE. (*Taking hold of PITTY herself.*) Sit down, love.

PITTY. (*Struggling.*) No! Let go! Look! There!

WINNIE. (*Covering her up.*) There's nothing there, love. You'll catch cold.

PITTY. I was whipped!

WINNIE. Yer got a keep warm.

PITTY. It's boilin' in'ere!

WINNIE. You'll miss yer tea.

PITTY. I wan' it now.

WINNIE. All right, I'll get it. 'Old 'er. somebody.

(*No one moves. WINNIE leaves PITTY and gets the tea.*)

PITTY. You musn't give her any. (*MADGE.*)

WINNIE. No.

MADGE. Why not? What've I done?

CHARLOTTE. She's your baby an' er're left 'oldin' 'er.

PITTY. No!

WINNIE. It's me 'oo's doin' the 'oldin'.

PITTY. Madge is bad.

WINNIE. None fer Madge, Pitty. Look, none fer Madge.

MADGE. This is daft. I'm not missin' a brew jus' t' 'umour 'er.

WINNIE. You'll do whass necessary!

MADGE. She's off 'er 'ead!

CHARLOTTE. Yer mean, she weren't before?

MADGE. I'm not takin' the blame.

SARAH. You can miss one cup.

MADGE. It's me 'oo looked after 'er. You lot cou'nt care less.

WINNIE. We're cryin' our eyes out, Madge.

MADGE. Jesus! (*She puts her head in her hands.*)

CHARLOTTE. Yer got what yer wanted.

MADGE. (*Up again, hysterical.*) An' this is justice, is it? Throw a tantrum an' the world's at yer feet?

WINNIE. It's nothin' t' do with justice, Madge. If those of 'oo can don' 'old t'gether now, we'll all be climbin' up the wall. (*She gives PITTY tea.*)

PITTY. Thank you.

MADGE. What a joke!

WINNIE. Spare us your fuckin' sufferin', thass all. We don't need it. Yer got nothin' t' complain about.

MADGE. I'm glad you think so.

WINNIE. Nance. (*She gives her tea.*)

NANCE. Ta.

(*The SURGEON comes in, let in by TOMMY, who stands at the door with a bucket of hot water. SURGEON says nothing but goes immediately to NANCE. They all watch. WINNIE continues with the tea.*)

SURGEON. Lie down. (*He pulls the remainder of NANCE's shirt away and examines her back.*) Let's have that water.

(*TOMMY gives him the bucket.*)

CHARLOTTE. Worthy a your professional skill, is it.

SURGEON. Listen here. During the Second Convict Fleet's voyage to New South Wales floggings like these caused more deaths than disease. It's senseless under these conditions, and practiced on women it's sheer barbarism.

WINNIE. Why don't yer stop it then?

(*NANCE yells as the SURGEON bathes her wounds.*)

NANCE. Oi!

SARAH. 'E'd lose 'isself a job.

CHARLOTTE. 'Sides, we're the real barbarians, ain't we.

NANCE. Oi!

SURGEON. (*To NANCE.*) Stretch your arms above your head. Straight out. Hold this. (*He gives her the broom. To CHARLOTTE.*) You're talking nonsense.

CHARLOTTE. She knocked the Sergeant's teeth out, didn't she?

SURGEON. It might've made my job easier if she knocked off the whole head. That would've saved me at least the work on the heads he's likely to knock off between here and Sydney. But then somebody would've asked me to fix his back on too. (*He applies ointment to NANCE's back and binds it.*) Heads are valuable, you see. The Captain's paid for not only every head that leaves England, as with the Second Convict Fleet, but a further four pound ten for every head that reaches Sydney. An incentive to be humane. The Sergeant's head therefore, since he's paid to stop you knocking each other's—or even our—heads off, is worth perhaps the entire cargo.

CHARLOTTE. An' whass your 'ead worth?

SURGEON. His and yours together, I suppose.

WINNIE. 'Oo to?

SURGEON. The Captain. I'm paid to keep both on.

WINNIE. What for? The fun of it?

(*SURGEON looks at her.*)

WINNIE. What else is there?

SURGEON. You've heard of humanity, I presume.

WINNIE. Sure. Only we're never included.

NANCE. 'Oo's side you on, doctor?

SURGEON. Neither.

WINNIE. That case yer can't 'elp us.

SURGEON. That's a matter of opinion.

NANCE. 'Elp keep us down p'raps.

SURGEON. You want treatment don't you?

NANCE. I wan' a cure.

CHARLOTTE. (*Pause.*) What yer goin' a do when yer get t' Sydney?

SURGEON. I've insisted my passage home be paid for. I've known friends be stuck two or three years in Australia through lack of means to return. Of course, if I found employment for the journey back, that means I'd be paid twice.

SARAH. Soun's like a good fiddle.

CHARLOTTE. Better'n thievin'.

SARAH. Safer an' all.

SURGEON. It's no more than we deserve. By comparison with other forms of opportunism on this run, it's nothing. I'm afraid you don't know the half of it.

CHARLOTTE. What is it to 'ave education, eh. Why don't yer come down 'ere one night, doctor? See what we can teach you.

SURGEON. If she develops a fever, call me. I'll come by every day and change her dressing. (*He goes out.*)

MADGE. Didn't work, did it.

CHARLOTTE. Shut yer face.

WINNIE. All that excitemen' on top a fresh air's made me tired.

CHARLOTTE. It's too bloody 'ot, thass the trouble.

SARAH. Thass the Surgeon done that to yer.

CHARLOTTE. Shut up.

SARAH. One thing about this place, yer can always catch up on yer sleep.

CHARLOTTE. Stop boastin'.

WINNIE. I thought you were off 'im.

CHARLOTTE. She is. Till tonight.

SARAH. 'Ave t' earn it if 'e wants it t'night.

PITTY. STUPID, SILLY TALK!!

MADGE. (*Pause.*) Thass it. (*She picks up her things.*)

PITTY. Whass she doin'?

(*MADGE crosses over to WINNIE and stands in front of her.*)

PITTY. Where's she goin'?

MADGE. I wan' a change.

PITTY. Madge!

WINNIE. Yer're jokin'. (*Pause.*) Yeh, all right. You look after Nance. (*She gathers her things.*)

PITTY. Please, Madge, please!

CHARLOTTE. Fer Christ's sake, Pitty, yer're not exactly in solitary!

PITTY. She's gone.

(*WINNIE crosses over to MADGE's place.*)

PITTY. I don't want you. I wan' Madge.

WINNIE. Yer're not gettin' no one.

(*PITTY gives a short, petulant scream, then grizzles.*)

CHARLOTTE. If yer don't shut up, Pitty, I'll cut yer soddin' tongue out.

WINNIE. She don't need that!

CHARLOTTE. Jus' cos you're lumbered with 'er!

WINNIE. I ain' liftin' a finger for 'er.

CHARLOTTE. Shut yer noise then.

WINNIE. Don' tell me what t' do!

CHARLOTTE. Don't tell me what she needs an' don' need then!

SARAH. Shut up, the pair of yer! It's worse'n fuckin' bedlam!

CHARLOTTE. Don't you interfere.
SARAH. I AIN' INTERFERIN'!
NANCE. (*Pause.*) Christ.

(*Pause. SARGE and TOMMY appear.*)

SARGE. Whass all the noise for?
CHARLOTTE. Sod off.
SARGE. Civil question.
SARAH. Rude answer.

(*SARGE and TOMMY come into the cell.*)

SARGE. Shame. I got good news for yer too.
WINNIE. Get 'im out of 'ere.
SARAH. Whass this good news? Settin' you adrift in an open boat, are they?
SARGE. Listen. The Captain's come up with a nice idea t' stop yer gettin' bored an' cantankerous durin' the journey. Somethin' to' keep yer minds occupied 'stead a tearin' each other t' pieces or takin' it out on me.
WINNIE. Get stuffed.
SARGE. Chain' er up.
SARAH. You can't do that!
SARGE. Button it then! (*Pause.*) All right. I'ave orders from the Captain t' supply those 'oo wan' it with cotton, needles an' material t' make shirts in their spare time. (*Pause.*) Well?

(*NANCE raises her head.*)

NANCE. Shirts fer 'oo?
SARGE. You shut up.
NANCE. Fer you?

SARGE. We got ours.

WINNIE. Fer us?

SARGE. Yours are special.

SARAH. Yeh, specially itchy.

WINNIE. If we make 'em, they're ours.

SARGE. You're paying fer the material, are yer?

NANCE. You payin' fer our labor?

WINNIE. They flog 'em when they get t' Van
Diemen's Land. My Mum tol' me.

(*NANCE sinks back again.*)

SARGE. Those 'oo wan' a make shirts collect the
materials from the Purser after lunch.

SARAH. Lunch 'e calls it!

SARGE. Those int'rested?

WINNIE. Calculatin' 'is bleeding profits already, the
bastard.

SARGE. T'day won' 'elp, yer know.

WINNIE. Nor you. Thass the main thing.

SARGE. Open up!

(*TOMMY opens the door.*)

MADGE. I'll do it.

WINNIE. (*Turning sharply.*) Whaffor?

SARGE. One. Any more?

(*PITTY raises her hand.*)

SARGE. Thass better. Any more?

WINNIE. Jus' fuck off out of it.

SARGE. Two then.

(*He goes to go. CHARLOTTE and SARAH raise their hands.*)

SARGE. Four.

(*He stands there. No response. He and TOMMY go.*)

WINNIE. (*To MADGE.*) What yer do that for?
MADGE. Yer get bored.
WINNIE. Thass nothin' new.
MADGE. Always tear 'em up again after.
CHARLOTTE. Yer won't though. They'll punish yer.
MADGE. So what? I'm sittin' in a floatin' fuckin' birdcage. I'm underfed, me limbs are stiff, the conversation's pitiful an' I'm bored t' tears. They can't make it worse'n that.
WINNIE. Whass that then? (*She indicates NANCE. Pause.*)
SARAH. 'E say we get scissors?
MADGE. No.
SARAH. Scissors be useful. Needle an' thread. We could patch ourselves up a bit. Make ourselves look nice.
CHARLOTTE. All right fer you. You got some int'rest.
SARAH. Once we got the tools, we can do what we like
WINNIE. Wan' a bet?
SARAH. Nick a couple fer ourselves.
NANCE. Pickin' us off one by one. Readin'. Sewin'. We'll be playin' the bloody piano next.
SARAH. Why not?
NANCE. Rowin' all the time. Hysterics. We 'ad some fuckin' dignity when we came in 'ere.
SARAH. Still got that
NANCE. I can't see it.

CHARLOTTE. I cou'nt see it then.

(*WINNIE who is standing, lurches.*)

WINNIE. 'Ere!
MADGE. Whass the matter?

(*Water splashes on CHARLOTTE.*)

CHARLOTTE. Oi!
SARAH. Whass goin' on?
CHARLOTTE. Look, wet on me arm!

(*Water splashes on MADGE.*)

MADGE. Oi!
WINNIE. (*Holding on to keep upright.*) What is this?
PITTY. We're sinking! We're sinking!
WINNIE. Shut up, Pitty. "Eavy water, thass all. It's the weather. Funny. Yer forget yer're on a ship.

(*Water splashes on MADGE again.*)

MADGE. Sod that. I'm movin'.
PITTY. Shou'nt a changed places, should yer.
MADGE. You shut up.

(*The boat lurches.*)

CHARLOTTE. Oi! What the fuck's goin' on? Where's Tommy?
WINNIE. 'E said there'd be a storm. (*Water drips on her.*)
WINNIE. Oi! Look, it's drippin' everywhere!
PITTY. We're leakin'! We'll sink!

CHARLOTTE. From the top down?
PITTY. HELP!!
CHARLOTTE. Shut 'er up, Winnie.

(*WINNIE holds her hand over the struggling PITTY's mouth.*)

CHARLOTTE. (*To SARAH.*) Give 'im a shout.
SARAH. Tommy!
CHARLOTTE. Oi!
SARAH. Tommy!
CHARLOTTE. Oi, we're gettin' wet down 'ere!

(*Regular dripping from all parts of the ceiling. Occasionally water splashes in quite hard.*)

MADGE. Eagh look, my bed's soaked.
CHARLOTTE. Move it then.
SARAH. Tommy!
MADGE. It's gettin' in everywhere.
CHARLOTTE. Where are they?
MADGE. Gone off an' left us, I bet.
CHARLOTTE. You're worse'n 'er.

(*PITTY, who sags as WINNIE lets go of her. Water splashes on CHARLOTTE.*)

CHARLOTTE. Oi! Yer think they'd make boats water-tight, wou'nt yer. I mean, of all things. They been makin' 'em long enough.

(*Water splashes on her again.*)

CHARLOTTE. Oi!
MADGE. Free shower, Charlotte.

SARAH. She needs it an' all.
WINNIE. I thought it was me 'oo ponged.
SARAH. You're not the only one.
CHARLOTTE. It's their subtle way of tellin' us.
SARAH. Where are they?
CHARLOTTE. Oh look, I'm bloody drenched.
WINNIE. Oi! What about some soap, then?
SARAH. Tommy!
WINNIE. Whass keepin' 'im?

(*They stumble as the boat lurches. Silence.*)

WINNIE. Quiet, en it.
CHARLOTTE. I can't 'ear a thing.
WINNIE. They 'ave gone, yer know.
SARAH. We're not goin' a sink are we?
CHARLOTTE. OI! TOMMY!

(*Silence.*)

CHARLOTTE. 'Allo! Anyone there?

(*Silence.*)

CHARLOTTE. TOMMY!

(*Silence.*)

SARAH. Got in the boats an' pissed off. Jus' like men.

(*The boat lurches. Silence. Water splashes in. Silence. NANCE starts tapping her mug with her spoon. The others join in. They chant 'Oi, oi, oi, oi, oi', rhythmically. PITTY makes a shrill keening noise*)

*above it. The sound is deafening. Eventually TOMMY
opens a hatch above the cell.)*

TOMMY. Whass the matter?

(He isn't heard.)

TOMMY. WHASS GOIN' ON?

(The noise breaks down. PITTY whimpers.)

CHARLOTTE. Where've you been?
TOMMY. Whass all the shoutin' for?
SARAH. We been callin' yer.
TOMMY. What for, though? I'm busy.
CHARLOTTE. Whass 'appenin'?
TOMMY. It's a storm, all 'ands needed. I can't stay.

*(The ship lurches. TOMMY slips. Water splashes in
through the hatch. His legs dangle into the cell.)*

PITTY. Come an' join us? Come an' join us!
TOMMY. Shut up. That ain' funny.
SARAH. You all right?
TOMMY. Could a been nasty.
SARAH. Not ruined, are yer.
TOMMY. Makes no different t' you, does it.
SARAH. I didn't mean that before.
TOMMY. I ain' goin' a be much good tonight anyway
if this lot keeps up. Bloody murder up 'ere.
MADGE. No fuckin' tea party down 'ere.
TOMMY. See yer later. *(He closes the hatch.)*
SARAH. Tom. *(She retches.)*
CHARLOTTE. Yer're not startin' that again?
SARAH. Fuck it. *(She vomits.)*

CHARLOTTE. All we needed.

Scene 9

Above the cell.
SURGEON, SARGE and the CAPTAIN, behind a table.

SURGEON. I'm sorry, I can't allow it.

CAPTAIN. It's not a question of what you'll allow, doctor. There's a hundred of those girls. They'd cut our throats as soon as look at us. I want to get to Sydney in one piece.

SURGEON. There's no question of mutiny.

CAPTAIN. There has been before and there will be again.

SURGEON. Not on this ship.

SARGE. Be foolish to underestimate 'em, sir. Only takes the slightest incident.

SURGEON. And what do you call a flogging?

SARGE. A deterrent, sir. What she did was a public display a rebellion. It 'ad t' be answered.

SURGEON. It'll be a month before those wounds heal.

SARGE. All the better, sir. Sort of reminder.

SURGEON. When I came aboard this ship we agreed I should have complete authority in all matters concerning the punishment of the prisoners.

CAPTAIN. Authority over the Sergeant, doctor. Not over me.

SURGEON. I wasn't consulted!

SARGE. It's my fault, sir, I wasn't aware a the position. I'm sorry.

CAPTAIN. In future we'll consult you, doctor.

SURGEON. That's not enough! You're breeding worse violence than you started with.

SARGE. Sir, listen, they look t' me fer a norm. You got a understan' that. What goes an' what don't go. Without me it'd be trial an' error, an' then where are yer?

SURGEON. I shall make a full report of this flogging, which I consider unnecessary. And if, after this conversation, I am not consulted in future on all matters of punishment, I shall make an official complaint to the Commissioner in Sydney.

SARGE. Fair enough.

CAPTAIN. I'd be grateful though too, doctor, if in future you'd exercise your skills with a little less self-righteousness and a little more concern for the welfare of the ship as a whole.

SURGEON. I don't presume to see the whole, Captain. I have a professional skill. What I see is from that perspective. It's precisely the fault of your perspective that you do presume to see the whole. Good day. (*He goes.*)

SARGE. I'll go careful then.

CAPTAIN. Consult him and avoid extremes. He has no power. I just don't want him bleating at me every other day.

SARGE. Yes, sir.

Scene 10

In the cell. Early morning.
PITTY's body hangs from the ceiling. Everyone is asleep.
CHARLOTTE stirs, sees the body. She wakes SARAH, points. They both stare. They speak softly. Dialogue slow throughout.

SARAH. Fuckin' 'ell.
CHARLOTTE. Like a side of beef.
SARAH. Wake the others.
CHARLOTTE. Too early.

(*SARAH sits up, feels the air.*)

SARAH. Yeh.

(*She settles back to sleep. WINNIE is woken by her movement. She sees the body and screams. The others wake. SARAH sits up again.*)

SARAH. (*To WINNIE.*) D'you 'ave to?
MADGE. She finally did it.
SARAH. Took 'er time.
CHARLOTTE. Puts 'er our of 'er misery, anyway.
NANCE. Four poun' ten more up the Captain's shirt.
CHARLOTTE. Better call the Guard.
NANCE. Too early.
SARAH. Tommy?
TOMMY. Leave 'er. She ain' doin' no 'arm. Get some sleep.
NANCE. (*Pause.*) I watched 'er. She got out a bed. Climbed on the stove. Slung the shirts over the beam. Kicked out. Like a swimmer.
WINNIE. You saw 'er?
SARAH. (*Pause.*) Call the Guard, Tom.
TOMMY. I'm not 'ere officially.
MADGE. Makes no difference. She knew what she was doin'.
WINNIE. Fuckin' 'ell.
CHARLOTTE. (*Loud.*) We goin' a sit 'ere an' watch 'er then?
WINNIE. It's too early.

CHARLOTTE. Don't be daft.

MADGE. I tried to 'elp 'er. I cou'nt do no more. She was a child. She didn't know what I was feelin'. I killed 'er.

NANCE. Bollocks.

SARAH. We sleepin' on or what?

CHARLOTTE. Make some tea, Win.

WINNIE. Someone else.

(*SARAH puts the kettle on.*)

NANCE. (*To TOMMY.*) You'd better get back.

TOMMY. I'll 'ave a tea first. Got any tobacco?

NANCE. Smoke yer own.

(*He does. Pause.*)

SARAH. Gets 'otter every day.

TOMMY. Thass the tropics.

SARAH. We could a done with them shirts. Mine's stinkin' already.

TOMMY. Wash 'em again Friday.

SARAH. Thass another 'alf-week.

CHARLOTTE. Fer Christ's sake, she killed 'erself!

NANCE. Stupid, en it.

WINNIE. She didn't 'ave to.

NANCE. Like I say.

TOMMY. (*Pause. To SARAH.*) Always take yer shirt off. I don't mind.

SARAH. 'Ave 'alf the crew outside the door.

TOMMY. Charge admission.

MADGE. You've changed in four months.

CHARLOTTE. (*To TOMMY.*) What d'yer think we are?

TOMMY. Comes natural to you lot.

(*CHARLOTTE clumps him.*)

TOMMY. Whass that for?

CHARLOTTE. I've 'ad enough a your cheek. We ain' made a lead.

TOMMY. Thass 'er privilege, not yours!

CHARLOTTE. I'm 'er mate.

TOMMY. I didn't think you were anyone's mate.

NANCE. Piss off, Tommy, you'll make yourself unpopular, I wan' a wash.

TOMMY. I can finish me fag, can't I?

NANCE. Yer're 'ere on suffrance as it is. Don't 'ang about. (*Pause.*) Get someone t' get rid of it.

SARAH. It's in my way.

WINNIE. Stinks bad enough as it is.

TOMMY. Give us time t' get back then start shoutin'. (*He gets up, looks at the body then gives it an irreverent but friendly swing.*) See yer, Pitty.

MADGE. (*Jumping up.*) Little cunt!

(*TOMMY darts outside the door and closes it.*)

NANCE. 'E's changed all right. (*She starts washing.*) Unlike the water.

CHARLOTTE. Sit down, Madge.

(*MADGE sits. Pause.*)

WINNIE. Thass an 'our's kip we lost t'day. Consistent t' the last, that girl. Used t' be 'er moanin' kept us awake.

(*NANCE smashes the cloth into the bucket.*)

NANCE. They fuckin' killed 'er! She should never a come on this fuckin' trip! That soddin' surgeon ought a be fuckin' castrated!

WINNIE. Nance, Nance.

NANCE. It makes me fuckin' mad.

WINNIE. Nance.

NANCE. I'll do 'im when 'e comes down 'ere, I'll fuckin' murder 'im!

MADGE. None of us 'elped.

NANCE. We ain' t' blame! 'Ow come it's our fault? We need 'elp ourselves.

SARAH. You finished?

(*NANCE leaves the bucket. SARAH washes.*)

WINNIE. Time we 'ollered, en it?

(*NANCE crosses quickly to the door. She yells.*)

NANCE. OI!!

(*The others join in 'Oi, oi, oi, oi, oi'. This continues till TOMMY comes back, casually.*)

TOMMY. All right, all right, I 'eard yer. I know already don' I.

(*They continue their chant regardless.*)

TOMMY. Fuckin' 'ell.

(*He goes. MADGE and WINNIE break away from the group at the door. The others go on chanting. WINNIE makes the tea. MADGE looks at PITTY. She clasps her*

*round the legs and puts her face against them. She
closes her eyes. She moans softly.)*

WINNIE. Madge.

(MADGE doesn't hear.)

WINNIE. Madge.

*(She still doesn't hear. WINNIE gives up. The others stop
their chant, invigorated.)*

CHARLOTTE. Where's that tea, girl?
WINNIE. Drawin'.
CHARLOTTE. She all right? *(She indicates MADGE.)*
NANCE. Leave 'er.

*(MADGE lets go of the body. She sits in a corner, head
down.)*

SARAH. They're comin'.
WINNIE. I'll pour the tea.

*(The others sit, SARGE, SURGEON and TOMMY arrive,
the first two in some haste.)*

SARGE. Open up!
NANCE. See what you done? Yer miserable little
murderer.
SARGE. I don't wan' none a your lip.
NANCE. You ain' buttoned it yet. Yer barreled me.
Locked me in the dark, poured water on me, whipped me,
an' yer still ain' shut me up. Yer shut 'er up, though. She
was easy.
SURGEON. Cut her down, sergeant

CHARLOTTE. (*To SURGEON.*) You're no fuckin' better.

SARAH. Our shirts a yours, sergeant.

SARGE. I noticed.

SARAH. Nice idea the Captain 'ad, eh.

(*SARGE and TOMMY lay PITTY on a bed. SURGEON examines her. SARGE collects up the shirts.*)

CHARLOTTE. The only sure diagnosis, en it. We told yer she was sick. What did you do? Nothing! You ought a be up there, not 'er.

SARAH. Murderer.

(*WINNIE trips SARGE up as he goes round collecting up the shirts. He goes to turn on her. All the girls stand. SURGEON finishes his examination. Pause.*)

CHARLOTTE. (*To SARGE.*) Got 'em all?

SURGEON. Sergeant.

(*SARGE and TOMMY carry PITTY out.*)

CHARLOTTE. I'll report the lot of yer when we get t' Sydney!

NANCE. Tell 'em that now, they'll 'ire an assassin t' shut yer mouth.

CHARLOTTE. Take more'n that now I got started.

NANCE. Took yer time though, didn't yer.

WINNIE. Cards?

CHARLOTTE. (*Pause.*) Where you been, Win?

WINNIE. I ain' played fer weeks. I'm gettin' rusty. Yeh?

CHARLOTTE. No.

WINNIE. Anyone?

NANCE. We don't need distraction, Win. They're in the wrong an' we're together. Thass real. Cards is silly.

WINNIE. All right. (*Pause.*) Bloody 'ot though. (*Pause.*) We got a do somethin'.

CHARLOTTE. I wonder if she was Pitt's daughter.

MADGE. (*Pause. Sings.*)**

DON'T ASK ME WHO I AM, MY FRIEND,
MY ANSWER IS A LIE.
FOR I MAY THINK I'M ANOTHER MAN,
AND TOMORROW I MAY DIE,
DON'T ASK ME WHO I LOVE MY FRIEND,
MY ANSWER IS A LIE.
FOR THE OTHER MY LOVE MAY NOT BE ENOUGH,
AND TOMORROW I MAY DIE.
DON'T ASK ME WHY I FIGHT, MY FRIEND,
MY ANSWER IS A LIE.
FOR I CAN'T KILL THE OTHER MAN'S RIGHT,
AND TOMORROW I MAY DIE.
THE SHIP WE SAIL ISN'T STRONG, MY FRIEND,
TO THINK SO IS A LIE.
IF IT SAILS US NOW, IT WON'T BE FOR LONG,
AND TOMORROW WE MAY DIE.

(*Long silence.*)

NANCE. Cheerful.

(*Long silence. WINNIE takes a shirt from under her bedding.*)

** Samuel French, Inc. regrets that it cannot supply sheet music for this song. If producers cannot locate music, they are hereby advised to compose music of their own.

WINNIE. Anyone wan' a shirt?
NANCE. Crafty!
CHARLOTTE. Too 'ot.

(*Long silence. TOMMY comes in, carrying two buckets and a mop. They look at him.*)

TOMMY. Fumigation.
CHARLOTTE. We only 'ad it last week.
TOMMY. They're steppin' it up. 'Count a the 'eat. An' the body.
NANCE. Last time the stink stayed fer days.
TOMMY. Be with yer all the time now. Mind yer feet!

(*He starts swabbing down, messily, splashing a lot. WINNIE grabs his arm.*)

WINNIE. Jus' wait a minute.

(*The others collect their things from the floor and sit up on the beds. TOMMY starts again.*)

NANCE. Get any a that on me, I'll tip the bucket on yer.
TOMMY. You try it, I'll fumigate yer fuckin' fanny for yer.

(*He mocks threatens her with the broom. CHARLOTTE brings her two fists down together on TOMMY's back. He goes down in the wet.*)

CHARLOTTE. 'Oo d'yer think you are, sonny?
TOMMY. Ah fuck. All over me.
CHARLOTTE. We're not 'ere fer your amusement, yer know. Learn a bit a respect.

TOMMY. Fer Christ's sake; I was only playin' around'! I get bored too, yer know.

WINNIE. 'Ard luck, yer got more space t' do it in.

TOMMY. I bent me finger back.

SARAH. Ah-h.

TOMMY. You're supposed to be on my side.

SARAH. Only one side in 'ere, fella.

TOMMY. Mind yourselves then. (*He flails around with the mop.*)

MADGE. Don' stink no better'n last time.

TOMMY. Think you're 'ard done by, I got six a these t' do. Like yer got it fer blood by the end.

WINNIE. Dry it proper this time. We don' wan' wet feet. Gives yer chilblains.

TOMMY. In this weather?

WINNIE. Dry it proper.

(*TOMMY pauses in his work.*)

TOMMY. I'm sweatin' on it faster'n I'm dryin' it.

WINNIE. Poor ol' thing.

TOMMY. Fuck off. (*He starts work again.*)

CHARLOTTE. What about the walls?

TOMMY. Next time.

SARAH. Idle bugger.

TOMMY. You could do this. 'Stead a sittin' on yer backside all day.

CHARLOTTE. Not our place to.

NANCE. Can't say we don' know our place.

TOMMY. Thass enough.

SARAH. It's wet down 'ere.

TOMMY. Slavedriver. (*He dries it.*) Look, 'ere's a cloth. Do yer stove yerself. An' yer pots an' thing. Right? (*He offers the cloth. No one takes it.*) Give 'em a wipe.

(*No one offers.*) Oh come on. (*No response.*) I'll leave it 'ere.

(*He puts the cloth down on the stove. NANCE picks it up and gives it back to him.*)

TOMMY. Whass wrong with you lot?
SARAH. Piss off jailer.
TOMMY. Sod yer then

(*He picks up his things and goes. Silence. It is over-poweringly hot and smelly.*)

WINNIE. Faugh!
NANCE. Better'n a rottin' corpse.
CHARLOTTE. Open a window.
WINNIE. Ha-ha.
SARAH. Oi!
CHARLOTTE. Whass the matter?
SARAH. Felt something 'ot.
WINNIE. What?
SARAH. Look at that. It's black.
CHARLOTTE. Sticky.
SARAH. Where's it come from?
MADGE. Tar.
SARAH. What?
MADGE. Tar. Off the ceiling. It's the 'eat. Look, between the beams. It's meltin'.
WINNIE. We're fallin' apart.
NANCE. We ain'. It is.

Scene 11

Above the cell.
SARGE, SURGEON and the CAPTAIN, behind his table.

SARGE. Whass your game? I thought we was splittin' fifty-fifty.

CAPTAIN. The Surgeon here indicated to me the likely nature of his report to the Sydney Commissioners.

SARGE. Which is?

CAPTAIN. Not very flattering.

SARGE. (*To SURGEON.*) What for?

SURGEON. It seemed the right thing to do. To warn the Captain in advance. And for the prisoner's sake.

SARGE. (*To CAPTAIN.*) Makes no difference though, does it? I mean, we knew that before. 'E's got no power, you said.

CAPTAIN. If his report tallies with the prisoners', it could be inconvenient.

SARGE. An' fer that you cut 'im in?

CAPTAIN. I told him that since he was present at the decision to have the women make shirts, it was only reasonable he should receive a percentage of the proceeds from their sale.

SARGE. 'Ow much percentage?

SURGEON. Twenty.

SARGE. Ten from each of us?

CAPTAIN. I'll get fifty. You'll get thirty.

SARGE. We agreed equal shares!

CAPTAIN. The situation's changed.

SARGE. Why should I suffer? It's you 'oo wants 'is mouth shut, not me.

CAPTAIN. You come off even worse in his estimation than I do. I'm protecting you as well.

SARGE. I'm not 'avin' it.

CAPTAIN. It's that or nothing. I need a crew to go back with.

SARGE. (*To SURGEON.*) An' you're goin' with 'im are yer?

SURGEON. I don't want to stay in Australia.

SARGE. 'Oo does?

CAPTAIN. It was that which made his mind up, sergeant. Even twenty percent wouldn't have persuaded him on its own.

SARGE. Virtue gets its reward, eh.

SURGEON. The Captain made a favorable report from me the condition for my return home with him.

SARGE. An' fer me it's a cut in percentage.

CAPTAIN. I'm assuming you want to come with us.

SARGE. Make it 'ard on a fella, don't yer. (*Pause.*) What can I say?

CAPTAIN. Good. Anything else?

SARGE. Yeh. We've sighted Sydney.

(*He goes. The SURGEON stands there. Pause.*)

CAPTAIN. Everything has its compensations, doctor.

Scene 12

In the cell.
Tattered, exhausted, completely drained of all life.
CHARLOTTE, SARAH, MADGE and NANCE sit
around, listless. WINNIE tidies and cleans. It has
become a compulsion. MADGE occasionally pulls at
her clothes, straightening them, brushing them down.
NANCE has a bad cough. Long pauses between
speeches.)

CHARLOTTE. So?
SARAH. I'll 'ave it.
CHARLOTTE. What for?

(*No answer.*)

SARAH. It's 'is.
CHARLOTTE. So?
SARAH. I'll 'ave it.
CHARLOTTE. (*Long pause.*) What for, though?
SARAH. I wan' it.
CHARLOTTE. What for?

(*No answer.*)

SARAH. I'll keep it.
CHARLOTTE. Where?
SARAH. In prison.
CHARLOTTE. Won't let you.
NANCE. Seven years.
SARAH. I know. (*Pause.*) Nearer six now. I done nothin' but be sick on this boat.
NANCE. Get rid of it.
SARAH. No.
MADGE. Work camps.
SARAH. Don't care.
MADGE. Probably never see each other again.
CHARLOTTE. Thass a relief.
WINNIE. Just as well. For them.
NANCE. Can't say we ain' worked at it.
CHARLOTTE. Not splittin' us two.
NANCE. (*Pause.*) Report 'em all.
SARAH. Not Tommy.

NANCE. Fraternization. Interference with prisoner's menstrual cycle.

SARAH. Nicest screw I ever 'ad.

WINNIE. Always wondered why they called 'em that.

CHARLOTTE. (*Pause.*) Three dead.

SARAH. One in 'ere.

CHARLOTTE. Wonder if she was Pitt's daughter.

WINNIE. (*Pause.*) See your bloke, Nance?

NANCE. No idea.

WINNIE. 'S a big place.

MADGE. Your brother, Win?

NANCE. Too knocked about.

CHARLOTTE. 'Im too though.

NANCE. Probably.

WINNIE. Can't remember what 'e looks like.

(*TOMMY comes in. He goes straight to SARAH. They embrace.*)

TOMMY. All right?

SARAH. What do you think?

TOMMY. We'll be there soon.

SARAH. Yeh.

TOMMY. Captain wants me 't go back with 'im.

SARAH. Least yer're not stuck 'ere.

TOMMY. Sail again in a fortnight. I'm goin' a save up. It's good money.

MADGE. You wan' a enjoy yerself. Whole year a this?

TOMMY. Tradin' on the way back. See Japan. China. Africa or Spain fer sure.

CHARLOTTE. Then what?

TOMMY. Thought I'd come back. I got a see me Mum an' Dad first. Tell 'em I'm settlin'. If that's all right.

MADGE. What?

TOMMY. Australia.

WINNIE. Yer wan' a 'ave a good look first. It's all Army an' Navy there. Be no better off'n us.

TOMMY. (*To SARAH.*) Think they'll let yer off early? (*Pause.*) Couple a years. Get a good job.

WINNIE. 'E's proposin'.

SARAH. You're mad.

TOMMY. It's my kid.

WINNIE. Watchin' 'is investments.

TOMMY. I wan' a marry 'er!

SARAH. Don't be daft.

TOMMY. I do!

SARAH. I'll believe yer when yer come back.

TOMMY. Can't without a promise, can I.

SARAH. I can't promise nothin'.

TOMMY. I can look your people up if yer like.

SARAH. What people?

TOMMY. Get a few things t'gether. Other blokes do it.

SARAH. It's yer first trip, Tommy.

TOMMY. I'm serious. Yer got an uncle, en't yer.

SARAH. This (*the baby*) might kill me. Or the work camps. I'll ferget yer. You me. The kid won't know. Use yer loaf.

TOMMY. I am. The other's got t' start somewhere.

MADGE. What you talkin' about?

TOMMY. I ain' goin' on like this fer ever.

SARAH. Don' ask me t' stop yer, thass all.

TOMMY. I'll come back anyway.

SARAH. Up t' you.

TOMMY. An' you!

SARAH. I ain't free, am I.

TOMMY. I mean it, Sarah.

NANCE. Now you do.

MADGE. Thass not whass in doubt.

TOMMY. What yer reckon then?

(*No answer.*)

TOMMY. Eh?

(*No answer.*)

WINNIE. (*Friendly.*) Clear off, jailer.
TOMMY. Why?
MADGE. Leave 'er.
TOMMY. I got a 'ave an answer.
NANCE. Don' be fuckin' stupid. The next day's all we got.
TOMMY. I come in, full a 'opes. I walk out that big. (*He indicates.*) Every time.
NANCE. It ain' just us, yer know.
SARAH. Yer been bigger'n that, Tom I won' forget.
TOMMY. Thanks fer nothin'. (*He goes.*)
WINNIE. (*Pause.*) Never made your surgeon neither.
CHARLOTTE. I forgotten what it feels like.
WINNIE. Sometimes I feel turned inside out. (*Pause.*) The sand's so white at Sydney, the sun's so bright they say yer get blinded when yer get off.
NANCE. Anythin' fer a change.

(*The CAPTAIN comes in with SARGE. The girls ignore him.*)

CAPTAIN. Tomorrow we'll be on dry land. We've made exceptionally good time: a hundred and fifty-three days. We've kept the rigors of accident and disease to a minimum. This cell was unfortunate in the loss of one of its number, but no one was to blame. I shall be making a report to the authorities in Sydney on prisoners' conduct, and you'll be pleased to know I can speak well of most of you. You will have the chance to make your own comments to the Penal Commissioner when you arrive. For my own personal interest, if you do have any complaints or suggestions, I should be pleased to hear them. I shall be in my cabin this evening if anyone wishes to see me. Anyone? (*The Girls look at each other. Pause.*) No one. Good. A word about personal effects then. When you came aboard, your own clothes were taken from you, and you were issued special clothing for the journey. I've taken it upon myself to keep these clothes for you, and they will be returned to you before you go ashore. Lastly, you'll find the sun in Sydney very strong after your long period of confinement, and if you can, I'd advise you to improvise some form of protection for your eyes. Thank you.

(*He goes. SARGE with him. Pause.*)

WINNIE. Amazin'.

MADGE. 'E don' even know 'e's doin' it.

CHARLOTTE. Complain to 'im now, 'e puts yer down quick as a trouble-maker.

WINNIE. Some'll fall fer it.

NANCE. I'm done already. You could see that in 'is face.

WINNIE. I ain't.

NANCE. You reportin' 'im?

WINNIE. Why not?

CHARLOTTE. You ain't tellin' 'im though.

WINNIE. What d'you think? (*Pause.*) I'd cut 'is liver out fer tuppence.

NANCE. You've got distinctly nasty, you know that?

WINNIE. Followed your example, didn't I.

SARAH. Ain't none of us is nice now.

NANCE. Never needed it in the first place.

WINNIE. Know where we stand though. No misunder-
standin's.

SARAH. Shame they'll split us up.

NANCE. We're still 'ere.

SARAH. Not t'gether though.

NANCE. Just more space between us, thass all.

SARAH. What we goin' a do about it?

CHARLOTTE. What?

SARAH. This sun.

WINNIE. Make 'ats.

SARAH. What with?

WINNIE. What we got?

CHARLOTTE. Sod all as usual.

NANCE. Always nick something.

SARAH. Like what?

WINNIE. Whatever's goin'.

SARAH. What, though?

NANCE. What we need!

SARAH. 'Oo from?

NANCE. 'Ooever's got it.

SARAH. They ain' goin' like it though, are they.

(*The hatches are taken off. The cell is flooded with brilliant
sunshine. The girls duck their heads.*)

MADGE. Jesus Christ!

TOMMY. (*From above.*) There are. Lovely sunshine!

SARAH. We ain' ready for it!

TOMMY. Yer got ten minutes.

(*The Girls shade their eyes.*)

WINNIE. Blimey!

SARAH. What we goin' a do?

CHARLOTTE. Come on, you two. You got all the answers.

(*NANCE, head down, sits down, opens her pillow and empties. it.*)

SARAH. Yer can't do that, Nance!

NANCE. Captain's orders. Improvise, 'e said. (*She takes out her needle and thread.*) Yer got one a these, en't yer. Like that. (*She folds her pillow.*) Stuff it. (*She does so.*) Sew across there. (*She indicates, then puts her pillow-hat on.*) 'Ow about that? (*The others laugh.*)

SARAH. I got a better idea.

NANCE. You do it then.

(*Heads down, each improvises a hat from her pillow.*)

END OF PLAY

BOTANY BAY.

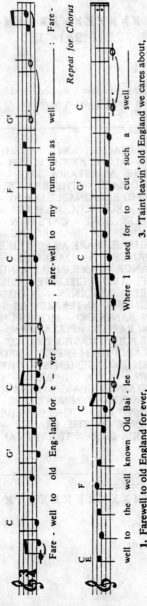

Repeat for Chorus

1. Farewell to old England for ever,
Farewell to my rum culls as well;
Farewell to the well-known old Bailee,
Where I used for to cut such a swell.

Chorus: Singing too-ral li-ooral li-ad-dity
Singing too-ral li-ooral li-ay;
Singing too-ral li-ooral li-ad-dity
Singing too-ral li-ooral li-ay.

2. There's the Captain as is our Commander,
There's the bo'sun and all the ship's crew,
There's the first and second-class passengers,
Knows what we poor convicts go through.

3. 'Taint leavin' old England we cares about,
'Taint cos we mispels what we knows,
But becos all we light-fingered gentry
Hops around with a log on our toes.

4. For seven long years I'll be staying here,
For seven long years and a day,
For meeting a cove in an area
And taking his ticker away.

5. Oh, had I the wings of a turtle-dove!
I'd soar on my pinions so high,
Slap bang to the arms of my Polly love,
And in her sweet presence I'd die.

6. Now, all my young Dookies and Duchesses,
Take warning from what I've to say,
Mind all is your own as you touchesses,
Or you'll find us in Botany Bay.

XXXXXXXXXXXXXXXXXXXXXXXXXXXXX

BURIED TREASURE FROM SAMUEL
FRENCH, INC.

Most of the superb plays listed below have never been produced in
New York City. Does this mean they aren't "good enough" for
New York? JUDGE FOR YOURSELF!

ABOUT FACE – AN ACT OF THE IMAGINATION -- ALL SHE
CARES ABOUT IS THE YANKEES -- ALONE AT THE BEACH --
AMERICAN CANTATA -- THE ANASTASIA FILE --
ARCHANGELS DON'T PLAY PINBALL -- THE BAR OFF
MELROSE -- BEDROOMS -- BEYOND REASONABLE DOUBT --
BILL W. AND DR. BOB -- BINGO -- BLUE COLLAR BLUES --
BODYWORK -- BRONTE -- CARELESS LOVE -- CAT'S PAW --
CHEKHOV IN YALTA -- A CHORUS OF DISAPPROVAL --
CINCINNATI -- THE CURATE SHAKESPEARE AS YOU LIKE
IT -- DADDY'S DYIN' -- DANCERS -- DARKSIDE --
ELIZABETH -- FIGHTING CHANCE -- FOOLIN' AROUND
WITH INFINITY -- GETTING THE GOLD -- GILLETTE -- THE
GIRLHOOD OF SHAKESPEARE'S HEROINES -- GOD'S
COUNTRY --- IMAGINARY LINES -- INTERPRETERS --
LLOYD'S PRAYER -- MAKE IN BANGKOK -- MORE FUN
THAN BOWLING -- OWNERS -- PAPERS -- PIZZA MAN --
POSTMORTEM -- PRAVDA -- THE PUPPETMASTER OF LODZ -
THE REAL QUEEN OF HEARTS AIN'T EVEN PRETTY -- RED
NOSES -- RETROFIT -- RETURN ENGAGEMENTS -- THE
RIVERS AND RAVINES -- ROBIN HOOD -- SHIVAREE -- A
SMALL FAMILY BUSINESS -- STAINED GLASS -- TAKE A
PICTURE -- TALES FROM HOLLYWOOD -- TEN NOVEMBER --
THEATER TRIP -- THIS ONE THING I DO -- THIS SAVAGE
PARADE -- TRAPS -- THE VOICE OF THE PRAIRIE --
WIDOW'S WEEDS -- THE WISTERIA BUSH -- THE WOMAN
IN BLACK

Consult our most recent Catalogue for details.
XXXXXXXXXXXXXXXXXXXXXXXXXXXXX